CAUTIOUSLY OPTIMISTIC

Essays Across the American Landscape

PETER FUNT

Published at Pacific Grove, California

Printed in the United States of America

Funt, Peter

    Cautiously Optimistic / by Peter Funt

    ISBN-13: 978-0615797014 (Candid Camera)

    ISBN-10: 0615797016

  1. Funt, Peter. 2. Commentary. 3. Candid Camera (Television program). 4. Journalism. 5. Media.

DEDICATION

For Amy:
In addition to helping with the editing on many of my op-ed columns, my wife Amy often stationed herself at a local coffee shop on the mornings when they first appeared in the paper, hoping to overhear kibitzing among readers. By making this disclosure, I believe the cost of her coffee and biscotti is fully tax-deductable.

CONTENTS

FOREWORD

I've always been fascinated by small slices of life.

During my time in broadcast and print journalism, as well as in entertainment television, I've looked for the smaller items that, when taken together, create a bigger picture of who we are and where we're headed.

On "Candid Camera," the landmark series created in 1947 by my dad, Allen Funt (first on radio as "Candid Microphone," and then a year later on TV), we showcased people "caught in the act of being themselves." While there are many memorable slapstick scenes in our library, the most meaningful vignettes, studied in college and high school classrooms around the world, are those that shed light on the human condition.

By the time the show suspended production—"hiatus" as we like to call it in TV, where formats never disappear completely, they just rest for a while—I had spent 20 years, producing and hosting nearly 200 network episodes.

In 2007 I decided to get back into print journalism, although it was only by accident that I wound up in the opinion section. Hillary Clinton had just launched her campaign for president and I noticed she was using only her first name. You had to look really hard to find the word "Clinton" anywhere in the "Hillary for President" materials, and I wrote 600 words about why this wife of the former president, herself a U.S. senator, was going the route of Beyonce, Cher and Madonna. To my surprise, *The New York Times* ran the piece as an op-ed.

I should have known from experience that this was a major case of Beginners Luck. Years earlier, after getting my journalism degree from the University of Denver, I was working at ABC News in New York and tried my hand at writing a feature article about a trend I had spotted in movies. It had to do with the fact that Hollywood was making films without the mandatory retribution for villains; it had become acceptable to have certain lovable crooks get away with their crimes. Sure enough it wound up in *The Times* Sunday Arts & Leisure section under the headline, "So They Robbed a Bank and Lived Happily Ever After."

My instant achievement in print was like the classic cartoon in which some character runs off a cliff and is doing fine in mid-air, until he's told, "Don't you know you can't do that!" whereupon he crashes to the ground. After a few more pieces in the Sunday *Times* my head was in the clouds and I became convinced that freelance writing was a gold mine. I quit my job at ABC—giving up my medical insurance and union benefits—to work at home as a newspaper and magazine writer. I never exactly crashed, but I soon began to understand how difficult it is to make a living as a freelancer.

I was getting pieces published in *The Times, The N.Y. Daily News and TV Guide*, among others, but it was hard to make ends meet. I took to delivering newspapers to supplement my income. I often wondered what my editor at *The Times* would have thought if he knew that the guy whose byline was in the Arts section was also selling the paper at night to people in bars and taverns. Come to think of it, an even odder occurrence would have been my asking someone, "Care to buy a paper? I've got an article on page 26."

Things changed for the better when a wealthy man who ran a regional cable-TV company, decided to invest in a monthly magazine of my invention called *On Cable*. This was the early '80s and the timing was perfect because many of the cable channels we're familiar with today—ESPN, CNN, USA, C-SPAN, etc.—were just getting started. Our circulation grew quickly to over 1.5 million. After five exhilarating years as editor and publisher, I sold the magazine to Cox Communications, whose brain trust then decided to close it down.

During all this I married Amy, a marketing manager at HBO, who showed up one day at *On Cable's* office to pitch the channel's latest programs. We soon had two kids, Stephanie and Danny, and moved from Connecticut to California.

The magazine's end marked the start of my work on "Candid Camera," collaborating with my dad and then taking over when he suffered a debilitating stroke. Doing the show was a great adventure, but it left little time for writing.

Which brings us back to 2007 and the Hillary Clinton op-ed. It seems that in my 20 years away from print journalism a lot had changed, not all of it for the better. For one thing, freelance writers were getting the same fees I had received decades earlier, and in some cases less. Newspapers were losing readers and revenue, resulting in cutbacks that affected all departments, including the opinion sections where I assumed I could, you know, successfully fly off a cliff.

But despite the mess I found in print media—a condition I'll get to later in this book—I managed to carve out a place for myself in a small corner of the op-ed world. My *thing*, as with "Candid Camera," turned out to be mostly under-the-radar observations generated while watching the world go by.

Many of the essays in this book were first published as op-ed columns in *The Times, The Wall Street Journal, Boston Globe, USA Today and The Washington Post*, while others were distributed by the Cagle Cartoon Syndicate. As I selected the material to include here, it occurred to me that my summary view could be described in the title *Cautiously Optimistic*. There's a lot wrong in the country—beyond the obvious matters of debt, war and political gridlock—but there remains plenty of good. On "Candid Camera" we celebrated the American spirit, and in the last five years of traveling, interviewing and researching, I'm happy to report that the spirit remains strong.

That said, my opinion pieces often focus on the negative. That's inherent in news and commentary; we don't dismiss all the good, but we search out those things that need to be fixed.

Just before this book went to press, there was an item in the news, plus a lot of online chatter, about people who work at home. That prompted a column that I'm presenting here to get things started, and to give you a picture of one freelancer's routine—even if it no longer includes delivering newspapers.

Home Free

As one who frequently works from home, I believe Yahoo's Marissa Mayer has seriously erred in decreeing that her staff will no longer be allowed that option, and will have to start showing up each day at the office. I've kept a diary of my productivity, and I'm forwarding this rundown of a typical day to Ms. Mayer, urging her to reconsider.

5:45 a.m.—Our dog Dorothy, who also works at home, insists we begin our day. I feed and walk her. Make coffee.

6:15—Retrieve the six daily newspapers from our driveway and place them in the kitchen on a pile that at times reaches three feet.

7:00—Monitor the "Today" show, flipping to "CBS This Morning" during commercials. As I've explained to my wife Amy numerous times, amateurs "watch" TV; media professionals "monitor" content.

7:10—Begin the tedious process of deleting emails that arrived overnight. These include various insurance offers, at least seven different summaries from Politico, plus dozens of other alerts and blogs I have signed up for over the years and can't seem to stop.

7:30—Wake Amy and warn that I've got a busy day and can't be interrupted.

7:45—Eat breakfast while using my iPad to check replays of what Jon Stewart and Stephen Colbert offered the night before.

8:30—Compose detailed emails to friends on the East Coast about pressing matters of the day, such as the NCAA basketball rankings, media layoffs, weather patterns across the West and various other things over which I have no control and won't likely recall at this time tomorrow.

9:10—Send out links to the best Stewart and Colbert bits.

9:30—Phone my mother to assure her that I'm fine, but too busy to talk.

9:32—Create lists of things I must do today, plus ideas for columns.

10:05—Check refrigerator for morning snack. Shower, shave, get dressed.

11:19—Drop everything. MSNBC has Breaking News about a private jet with eight people aboard that is approaching St. Louis with landing gear trouble.

11:37—After 18 minutes of uninterrupted coverage, MSNBC's Tamron Hall says the plane has landed safely. An "aviation expert" named Jim tells her it was a "non-story."

11:38—Check mailbox. Place bills on a pile in the kitchen that currently reaches five inches in height.

11:55—Check six Internet sites. Break for lunch.

1:35—Running behind because I apparently dozed off after lunch.

2:00—Text son Danny with news that Xavier Nady had two hits in a minor-league baseball game. Text daughter Stephanie that her law school tuition payment was delayed because I couldn't remember newest password for online bank account.

2:15—Begin writing column about how modern camera shots on TV news and talk programs make viewers dizzy because the camera keeps swinging in, out and around, sometimes making a full 360-degree turn. Seems like a solid start, but I'm stumped on what to do for the next 450 words.

2:45—Email fellow writers for thoughts about how to finish column.

2:50—Take afternoon break for jog at local high school track.

3:20—Check refrigerator.

3:30—Step out to fill car with gas, and pick up toothpaste at pharmacy.

3:50—Remove gas and toothpaste from to-do list. Shift other items to tomorrow's list.

4:00—Monitor "Hardball," followed by "Seinfeld" reruns.

5:01—Email editor that the column about TV camera shots is "coming along well."

5:05—Knock off for the day. However, thanks to the flexibility of working at home, I'll be able to remain on duty until bedtime.

WHO ARE WE?

Society Craves 'Respect'

After informing the airline customer-service agent on the telephone that she had made an error in my itinerary, I was taken aback by her reply. She said I had "disrespected" her.

A few days later I read about a small but telling incident aboard an Amtrak train traveling up the West Coast, involving a woman who talked incessantly on her cellphone in a so-called "Quiet Car." According to KATU television in Portland, passengers said the woman was being "disrespectful." Police finally removed her from the train, whereupon she told reporters that she felt "disrespected" by the entire incident.

Apparently "respect" has emerged as society's favorite go-to word when we don't like someone or something, or they don't like us. Listen closely to the patter of politicians and athletes, reality-TV stars and gang members; and you'd think all they want from life nowadays is to be respected.

Not since Rodney Dangerfield's prime ("I get no respect: When I was born the doctor slapped my mother") has there been so much blather about "respect" and "disrespect." One of John Boehner's early acts upon becoming House Speaker was to tell "60 Minutes" that President Obama had "disrespected" him. The alleged insult was the president's statement that Republicans were "holding hostage" middle-class tax relief while trying to win cuts for the wealthy.

Most of us are schooled in basic respect for elders, flag, clergy, courts and so forth. We were taught that respect was something that was earned. Somewhere along the line, however, the concept has been inverted. Respect is no longer measured so much by what we achieve as what we demand.

It's difficult to pinpoint the precise moment that a term takes on new meaning, but Aretha Franklin's 1967 anthem, "Respect," was an early indicator of this particular rhetorical shift. Back then, the song underscored reasonable goals of the civil rights and women's rights movements. Today, the concept of "respect" has been commandeered by those with far less laudable objectives.

In a report on California gang violence, the *Oakland Tribune* asked a police lieutenant why conditions are so bad. "It is usually some form of disrespect," he explained, "or inferred disrespect."

Understandably, those in the poorest circumstances have little to cling to if not self-respect. However, the misappropriation of the concept now extends from America's violence-torn neighborhoods to the halls of Congress. It resonates in modern music and is amplified by social networking.

Professional athletes, who command enormous power to influence the thinking and rhetoric of millions of Americans, are increasingly obsessed with the notion of "respect."

For example, after five seasons with the Titans, quarterback Vince Young declared that coach Jeff Fisher had "disrespected" him during the entire time he spent in Tennessee. When Donovan McNabb left the Philadelphia Eagles, several former teammates accused Mr. McNabb of disrespecting them. Then, when Mr. McNabb was benched by the Redskins, his new team, he said the coach, Mike Shanahan, was disrespecting him.

Writing in the *Detroit News*, Bob Wojnowski summed up the Pistons basketball season, saying it was marked by "nastiness, pouting and confusion." This, he concluded, was due to "a breakdown in respect for the game, respect for fans, respect for each other." He went on to note that the players showed a "lack of respect" for their coach and also disrespected the team's owner.

In baseball, the concept of respect has become so twisted that if a player dares celebrate a successful play he's in danger of being beaned his next time up because he "disrespected" the other team. And then there was Edgar Renteria, the 2010 World Series hero for the San Francisco Giants, who said the team showed a "lack of respect" and "total disrespect" by offering him only a million dollars to play in 2011.

Nearly 200 years ago, Webster defined respect as: "That estimation or honor in which men hold the distinguished worth or substantial good qualities of others." In the modern online Urban Dictionary, where entries are rated by readers, the leading definition of respect is: "A quality seriously lacking in today's society."

Sometimes in our living language we allow a good word to go bad, and in doing so redefine ourselves. Today, those most adamant in demanding respect are often the least likely to deserve any.

◆◆◆

Rise of the 1 Percent

What are the odds that you're part of the 1 percent? No not that 1 percent—folks who get so much attention because they earn more than $380,000 a year—but the nation's numerous other, less publicized factions of 1 percenters.

For instance, while 99 percent of Americans do not work at Walmart, the other 1 percent does. Walmart employs roughly 1.4 million people in its U.S. operations, or 1 percent of the work force, according to the Bureau of Labor Statistics.

All those warnings on snack packages are for the benefit of 1 percent of Americans who are allergic to peanuts.

Sometimes it seems we have an abundance of bureaucrats, but added together, they don't constitute more than 1 percent. The Census Bureau estimates there are 500,000 elected officials in the U.S., and even if you combine them with everyone alive who has ever held office, you still have, yes, about 1 percent.

Ninety-nine percent of Americans don't belong to a gang. However, the FBI now puts gang membership at 1.4 million, or about half of 1 percent of the total population. Gangs are one of the fastest growing segments of society, having increased by 40 percent in just the last three years—something the 99 percent should really be concerned about.

While income is the principal metric among those who decry "class warfare," a more profound distinction involves those who serve in the military. Shortly after assuming his post, Defense Secretary Leon Panetta praised the "men and women who represent less than 1 percent of our nation, but who have shouldered the burden of protecting the American people."

We hear a lot about undocumented immigrants, many of them from Mexico, but what's the situation on the other side of the border? Well, 99 percent of Americans don't live in Mexico but, surprisingly, quite a few do. In fact, there are one million American citizens living in Mexico.

The Census Bureau says there are now almost 2 million Americans older than age 90, making the super-aged a force to be reckoned with as they approach 1 percent of the population.

You're probably happy to have health insurance, or wish you had it, if you're among the 1 percenters who suffer from epilepsy, glaucoma, celiac disease, or type 1 diabetes.

Roughly half of 1 percent of Americans are Muslims. That's about the same percentage of Americans who are Buddhist.

According to government estimates, 99 percent of Americans do not go out dancing once a week, but exactly 1 percent of the adult population does. Ninety-nine percent of us don't play a musical instrument each week, or go to the beach, or attend an adult education class. But in all cases there is roughly 1 percent that does.

One percent of adults are in the under-publicized group that tries to complete a Sudoku puzzle each week, and we can thank government research for making us aware of that.

One percent of U.S. households don't have a radio. One percent of Americans still access the Internet with an AOL dial-up connection. One percent of American adults will buy a car or truck from General Motors this year—meaning, of course, that 99 percent will not.

It's us versus them, just like it's always been.

How Class Warfare Begins

There's class warfare in the U.S. all right. Good examples can be found at the nation's airports and on its highways.

California has replaced HOV (high occupancy vehicle) lanes on some major highways in Silicon Valley with what ought to be called HRL—High Roller Lanes. The idea is to raise money by allowing single-occupant vehicles to travel in the speedy carpool lanes, provided motorists are willing to pay a fee.

Instead of rewarding all citizens for carpooling to reduce congestion and pollution, the California approach means affluent drivers can ignore those concerns, while others—referred to lately as the 99%—must still carpool, or face lengthy delays in the poor people's lanes.

At airports, passengers with expensive tickets or elite status breeze through TSA checkpoints, while others wait in lines that are often quite long. Like highways, which are publicly owned and operated, airport security is a government operation that supposedly guarantees equal rights for all. Why are airlines allowed to sell premium customers the rights to faster government inspections?

Here's some free advice for needy, greedy government agencies (although for a fee, I'll send any bureaucrat my Premium Column, which has my really good ideas).

At public libraries, start selling gold and platinum cards in addition to giving out the ordinary, free library cards. Elite readers can keep books for twice as long as regular patrons, and get first crack at new titles when they arrive.

In public parks, set up Executive Lawn Space, where people pay a fee to romp on the cleanest, greenest, most carefully mowed grass, with Concierge Litter Removal. Regular users can sit in the less desirable spots and dodge the dog droppings at their own peril.

On public beaches, offer special areas for premium Beach Club members. For a fee, members receive a sticker that entitles them to spread their blankets in the best spots and be guaranteed a 10-foot spacing zone to keep away ordinary, nonpaying beachgoers.

There's no reason Washington can't get in on this to solve its money problems. Why not open a Red Carpet Club inside the Lincoln Memorial? How about charging for the best burial spots at Arlington National Cemetery?

Of course, the private sector is way ahead of government when it comes to segregating the classes. The best examples can be found at modern sports stadiums, where paying a higher price for a good seat is no longer enough. Affluent fans now park in better lots, enter separate gates, dine in different food areas, and—best of all!—are physically barricaded in their sections so that other fans can't even walk through.

Is it any wonder that with construction of each new stadium, fan rowdiness increases, causing even more segregation and thus more discontent?

Private business has the legitimate right to establish pricing by which customers pay more to get more (although you have to wonder what sort of scrutiny regarding fan fairness is being applied by municipalities when they authorize and help finance sports facilities). But government is supposed to operate differently.

Highway lanes for the wealthy and speedy airport screening for the rich are dangerous precedents. Politicians who truly oppose class warfare ought to stop coming up with schemes that encourage it.

♦ ♦ ♦

Profiling 2.0

E ver since 9/11, profiling has been a frequent subject of debate, as we look around and wonder if there are terrorists among us.

After decades of abuse, racial profiling of blacks may actually be in a slight decline—not enough, certainly, but moving in the right direction. Yet, other forms of profiling are increasing, in some cases with the government's encouragement.

Ask a U.S. citizen of Muslim faith, especially one favoring Middle Eastern dress, what it's like to travel by plane in post-9/11 America, and you're likely to hear plenty about profiling. Ask a Hispanic American about profiling after he or she is subjected repeatedly to unwarranted scrutiny about immigration status.

For that matter, ask an overweight person what it's like to be profiled by a maitre d'. Ask gray-haired people in their 50s, in perfect health and with excellent skills, if they believe there's a problem with age profiling by employers. Ask those with visible tattoos and piercings what types of unwelcome profiling come with body art.

It is true that as a nation of immigrants, America has always had to deal with some measures of ethnic, racial, and religious stereotyping. As a society, though, we like to think of ourselves as generally tolerant of those in our melting pot—but many factors make that assumption troublingly open to question.

Since 9/11, travelers in airports, train stations, and other public venues have been encouraged to profile those around them and to report anything suspicious. Even without instruction, most of us would be doing that anyway. Can you honestly say you've watched airline passengers coming down the aisle without relating their appearance and clothing to a profile that fits your fears?

This process is both sanctioned and practiced by government. The Transportation Security Administration now has more than 2,000 plain-clothed "behavior detection officers," whose mission is to profile people in airports, right down to their facial expressions and apparent levels of anxiety. The TSA won't say if anyone among the first 180,000 citizens detained under the program turned out to be a terrorist, but CBS News reported that none was found.

Many local and state police agencies teach profiling. Joe Arpaio, the notorious sheriff of Maricopa County in Arizona, is said to encourage his deputies to use skin color as a pretense for stopping suspected illegal immigrants—a charge under investigation by the Justice Department. Isn't there an inherent contradiction when government preaches against profiling, yet practices it at the same time?

And what about in the private sector? The car dealer profiles customers even before they move from the lot to the showroom. By the time the bell rings on the first day of class, the teacher has profiled each new student. I know a successful golf pro who insists he can profile a player's handicap index within three points, just by watching him take his clubs from his car and walk to the driving range. And no one should even try to compete in a singles bar without a degree in advanced profiling.

This is our nature. But in less stressful times, perhaps, we are better at curbing the worst aspects of that natural behavior.

Now, however, more profiling seems to be on the horizon. The decline of Caucasians as a percentage of total U.S. population, erosion of the middle class, extended life spans of older Americans—they all contribute to societal splits. With them come anxiety, suspicion and stereotyping. We are increasingly a nation of "us" and "them," and we tend to create negative profiles about "them."

The more we judge each other based upon a dubious list of presumed traits, and the more effort government devotes to employing the same tactics in the name of making us safer, the more it damages society's own larger profile.

◆◆◆

Hunting for Heroes

America's developing quite a thing for heroes—not the kind in fiction, but the real-life variety.

Oprah did entire shows about them. CNN ranks and profiles them in recurrent specials. President Obama even released a kids' book about his 13 favorite heroes, and presented the Medal of Honor to Army Sgt. Salvatore Giunta, the first time the award has gone to a living hero since Vietnam.

Several nonprofit organizations—including the Heroic Imagination Project, and the Giraffe Heroes Project—are dedicated not only to identifying heroes, but also to nurturing new ones. Some experts are convinced that heroism is, at least in part, learned behavior, and they argue that we need more of it.

While we loosely apply the term "hero" to athletes, entertainers and the generally rich and famous, the spotlight is shifting increasingly to ordinary folks. A classic example is the pilot Chesley Sullenberger, who, in 2009, managed to land safely in the Hudson River after his commercial jet hit a flock of birds. A few months later he threw out the first pitch at opening day in San Francisco, served as Grand Marshal at the Rose Parade, made dozens of TV appearances, and was exhaustively covered in a half-dozen books, including his own.

Captain Sully's experience proved he's an extraordinary pilot, but is he a hero? How about Wesley Autrey, the construction worker who jumped onto the tracks to save a young man who had fallen, and became known in media as New York's Subway Hero? Autrey risked injury or death, but was that a heroic act, or an impulsively foolish gambit?

One episode of "CNN Heroes" focused more on life-long pursuits. Among the people featured: a 74-year-old doctor who cares for as many as 900 patients a day in the crime-ridden town of Juarez, Mexico, at the hospital she helped start; a Cambodian man who planted thousands of land mines as a soldier, and now devotes his time to finding and removing them; a builder in Houston, Texas, who constructs mortgage-free houses for military vets.

The Giraffe Heroes Project, whose name relates to sticking one's neck out, has identified roughly 1,000 heroes at www.giraffe.org, such as the cheerleader from Iowa who creates cheering squads around the nation for students with disabilities. There's a Giraffe kit for schools, complete with hero trading cards and videos. The objective is underscored in the organization's slogan: "Encouraging today's heroes; training tomorrow's." But, hold on. Is that really possible?

Philip Zimbardo, the noted Stanford psychology professor and author, believes it is. "Heroism can be learned by example and reinforced with practice," he maintains.

Zimbardo heads up The Heroic Imagination Project. "The definition of a hero that I promote," he told me, "is someone who acts voluntarily on behalf of others in need, or in defense of a moral cause, aware of risks and costs, without expectation of tangible rewards."

Zimbardo (with whom I've worked on unrelated projects) seeks "a growing community of heroes, all empowered to initiate extraordinary social change."

Fundamental in Zimbardo's work is his assertion that risk need not be the major component of heroism. "Nobility of purpose and non-violent acts of personal sacrifice," are keys. Heroes include "those individuals who challenge institutionalized injustice, deception, and fraud."

Left unclear in the hunt for heroes is whether there are more such people today, or if our trying times, combined with a reality-TV mindset, simply make us more determined to find them. Maybe our ever-squabbling politicians, over-indulgent entertainers, and scandal-plagued business leaders have made us look elsewhere for people to admire.

"Heroes are created by popular demand," wrote the journalist Gerald W. Johnson. In these demanding times we could certainly use a lot more.

◆ ◆ ◆

SIZING UP MEDIA

Where's the Rub?

A group of daily papers in New England calls its electronic edition No Inky Fingers. The point, of course, is that with digital news nothing rubs off on readers' hands. But what's rubbing off on their brains?

The disappearance of what could be called the mental rub-off effect is partly to blame for the fact that many Americans are overloaded with information, yet seem to know less than ever about current events. As news packaging shifts from general interest to specific interest, it becomes difficult for mass audiences to rub up against the news—even if accidentally.

Not long ago most American homes received at least one daily newspaper. Just idly turning the pages to find the sports section or comics, readers couldn't help but glance at the news headlines, and bits of information tended to rub off.

Television, before cable and satellite, was arranged so that most entertainment stopped at the dinner hour and again before bedtime for general-interest news broadcasts. Just turning the dial, or waiting for the weather forecast, viewers couldn't help but sample a bit of hard news.

And think how radio used to be. The government basically required stations to run news or "public service" programming—so whether you were listening to rock, country or classical, every hour programs paused for a few minutes of news. My first job out of college was in the news department at WABC in New York back when it was still a rock 'n' roll powerhouse. Despite the likelihood that our audience resented it, we interrupted Cousin Brucie and the other DJs every hour for five minutes of no-nonsense news. Some listeners switched stations, but most stuck around—and the news rubbed off.

Walking down the streets of most cities back in the day, news was always nearby. It was stacked up at newsstands and even shouted by vendors. People carried transistor radios whose messages resonated in the pre-earphone era.

By contrast, today's boutique media allow many people to skip news altogether. You can set your Internet home page so that it serves up only what you're interested in. You can watch video via Hulu or YouTube and never encounter a smidgen of news. You can listen 24/7 to satellite radio or other digital music services and not be bothered by reportage from the outside world.

Even consumers who answer surveys by stating that they get "news" online or by watching cable channels often are referring to something that isn't really news at all. Some cable "news" channels devote virtually all of prime time to nonstop campaigns for liberal and conservative agendas, making little or no effort to summarize the major news of the day.

Many television producers and an increasing number of newspaper editors mistakenly believe that since the day's hard news is readily available, around-the-clock, from so many sources, it's no longer in their commercial interest, or the public interest, to serve it up themselves.

When I asked a college media class of 40 students if they read a daily newspaper, two hands went up. When I clarified that online newspaper sites qualified, three more hands were raised. Yet everyone in the class claimed to be at least generally aware of the news. I was told that "important stuff" gets relayed by text, tweet or other social media.

While that's often true, it contributes to the total inversion of the traditional process by which news is disseminated. Anyone who has ever worked in a newsroom is familiar with the most basic debate among journalists: Should we give the public what it wants to know, or what it ought to know? The best prescription has always been a combination of both.

However, the line that separates those considerations is moving—both because journalists are succumbing to competitive pressure, and because consumers are taking it upon themselves to alter the equation. Thanks to modern media and devices, they have the tools with which to change it.

The standard pushback is that there's more information out there than ever before, and that interested consumers want to sort through it to find the news. Again: Want? Or, ought?

The sad truth is, while some of us are naturally curious about what we don't know, an increasing number of readers and viewers want only reinforcement of what they already know. While it's not the job of media to force-feed news to an uninterested audience, the system worked better when some news and information just happened to rub off.

Personally, I've always relied upon great editors and great broadcasters to tell me what they think is important each day. I'm determined to form my own opinions, but I'm not so audacious as to think I know what's important without professional help.

One of my favorite news slogans is one used for decades by the Scripps newspaper chain: "Give light and the people will find their own way." Yet in modern communications we seem to give off more heat than light, leaving too many information-loaded consumers stumbling around in the dark.

◆◆◆

The Newswatch Never Stops

Soon after the Tucson shooting tragedy, *The New York Times* reported erroneously via its website that Rep. Gabrielle Giffords of Arizona was dead. Two things followed quickly. The first was a much-needed correction. The second was a renewed assertion among some print journalists that nonstop, 24/7 reporting—driven by the Internet—is perilous for news providers and puts responsible reporting in jeopardy.

The Washington Post suffered similar embarrassment in 2011 when its website reported that John Wooden had died, although at the time the legendary UCLA basketball coach remained alive. In the aftermath, one senior editor at the *Post* said the intense pressure of a never-ending deadline was "like walking on egg shells."

All this fussing by newspaper folks as they wake up to demands of the digital era is rather quaint. The Internet has made real-time reporting more prevalent, but it certainly didn't invent it.

All-news radio began in the early 1960s at stations like WAVA in Washington, D.C., and WINS in New York, where it was refined to become the nonstop reporting format that remains popular today. In 1980, media visionary Ted Turner launched CNN, and nonstop television news has been a vital part of American journalism ever since.

As it happened, the incorrect report about Rep. Giffords was actually generated by broadcasters at CNN and NPR, and was simply picked up by *The Times*. But while managers at CNN and NPR fumed over the mistaken facts—as they should—print veterans seemed equally determined to fault the process.

At first glance, the headline on *The Times's* own analysis of its coverage, "Time, the Enemy," made me wonder if the newspaper had some sort of quarrel with *Time* magazine. I never imagined that the "enemy" was time itself. Arthur Brisbane, the paper's public editor at the time, wrote that elements of the Tucson coverage "illustrate how difficult it is in the current environment to be both timely and authoritative."

Yet that has always been a challenge for journalists. Even publishing once per day, *The New York Times*, like *The Wall Street Journal* and most other papers, must regularly print corrections. Mistakes happen. Would there be fewer errors if newspapers came out weekly? Perhaps, but the extension of that argument is that the best way to avoid mistakes would be not to publish at all.

Parkinson's Law states that, "Work expands to fill the time available for its completion." Half a century ago the pioneers of all-news radio wondered about the converse: To what extent would the task of responsible reporting suffer as the time to accomplish it shrunk?

The answer lay in the definition of news itself. News is instantaneous. With the exception of the tree that falls in the empty forest, reporting begins at some level at the very moment that news happens. Professional journalists—whether print or electronic—are simply an extension of the process. All deadlines are artificial.

I recall going to work at the ABC Radio Network shortly after the company expanded from one newscast per hour to four; all of a sudden there was a deadline every 15 minutes. For many of us on the news desk this schedule was extremely difficult at first, because we felt that time had collapsed while the task of creating a finished five-minute newscast remained the same.

But colleagues working nearby at the all-news radio station were not similarly burdened. For them the pressure was removed, or at least sharply reduced, when there were no deadlines at all. On television, legendary coverage by Walter Cronkite and others during events such as the Kennedy assassination and the first moon walk—in the days before CNN and 24/7 TV news—demonstrated how deadlines could be measured by fact rather than time: Get it right and get it on. That was the schedule.

This is not to say that the power of the Internet to quickly disseminate errors is not cause for concern, as was the case immediately following the massacre in Newtown, Conn. Nor is the 24/7 news cycle an excuse for journalistic carelessness.

But the notion that nonstop news coverage is something new, some recent innovation developed as a product of the Internet and utilities such as Twitter, is bogus.

What newspaper editors could learn from broadcasters is that time need not be the enemy. It is integral to the very definition of news. Also, it waits for no journalist.

News Flash: Internet Rants Aren't News

The explosive growth of social media gives voice to millions, indeed billions, of people world-wide who might otherwise never be heard. Access to the Internet supplies the digital-age correction for a long-standing concern that distributing mass messages is possible for only the rich and powerful.

But conventional news outlets, enamored of Facebook and Twitter and eager to join their conversations, increasingly give space and credibility to online chatter that ordinarily wouldn't deserve either.

In December 2012, when a nurse at a London hospital hanged herself after being victimized by a phone prank originating at an Australian radio station, there was a torrent of opinion online. ABC News plucked two tweets from among thousands and ran them full-screen. One, aimed at the radio hosts, said, "You scumbag, I hope you get what's coming to you!" The other warned, "You have blood on your hands now."

Had such comments from the general public reached ABC News by any other method—from email to carrier pigeon—there is virtually no chance they would have been deemed newsworthy. Indeed, they probably would have been viewed as incendiary. Yet mainstream reporters increasingly treat social media as part of the story, conflating media with messages.

On television as well as on newspaper websites, anonymous tweets—sometimes in endless crawls at the bottom of the screen—have become staples. They fall short of the basic standards for author identification that most publications require for letters to the editor.

Some MSNBC programs present a barrage of Twitter messages that are more distracting than informative. One night, for instance, during coverage of a lawsuit by AIG shareholders against the government, one tweet informed viewers that "AIG is nothing but a bunch of greedy punks."

And mainstream producers could hardly contain themselves when the girlfriend of Alabama football star A.J. McCarron became an Internet sensation during the college title game. TV shots of Katherine

Webb prompted hundreds of thousands of people to follow her on Twitter, leading to even more TV coverage, which in turn triggered more tweets. It underscored the fact that relentlessly reporting social-media comments on trivial subjects has the effect of further trivializing them.

In a single program, NBC's "Today" show blurred things by including anonymous Internet posts in two stories that were, themselves, about media. The first concerned a decision by the *Journal News* newspaper to print the names and addresses of everyone with a legal gun permit residing in its coverage area north of New York City.

According to NBC's story: "One Facebook user writes, the paper is '. . . treating legal gun owners like criminals.' Another says, 'This is the most disgusting act of journalism ever.'"

Had NBC sent a reporter to conduct on-street interviews with people living in the area, the comments might have had some validity. But, in addition to being faceless and nameless, the Internet posts NBC chose to run could have come from anywhere in the world.

The second story focused on the sister of Facebook founder Mark Zuckerberg, Randi, who was miffed because her Facebook photo of a family gathering was tweeted globally without her permission. NBC again turned to an anonymous post saying, "If the Zuckerbergs can't even figure out Facebook's privacy settings, how are we supposed to?"

At least this post made sense, noting the irony of the Zuckerberg family being confounded by its own creation. Even more ironic is that Randi Zuckerberg serves on what NBC calls its Digital Advisory Committee. One piece of good advice she could give the news division would be to stop running anonymous comments from Facebook and Twitter. Another would be to refrain from retransmitting photos from the public that haven't been authenticated.

And, as a general rule regarding social media, stop awarding the prize of mass distribution to whomever is most outrageous.

◆◆◆

Cable's Lessons

At the end of the 1970s, CNN was just a twinkle in the eye of yachtsman Ted Turner, of all people. ESPN was on the drawing board at Getty Oil, of all places. HBO was helping Time Inc. confirm that consumers would pay for television content, of all things.

The emergence of cable and pay-TV programming marked an exciting and explosive stage in America's communications history. As we enter a similar period with the Internet and digital technology, it's worth reviewing what was learned from the video revolution three decades ago.

Of course, for each individual user of new technology the revolution starts when it reaches the doorstep. The World Wide Web has been around since 1992, and the computers it serves were invented several decades earlier. But for most consumers and businesses the real breakthroughs in accessing and marketing digital content are still on the horizon.

I first took note of cable's growth in a 1979 article (re-published in 2011 by the Harvard Business Press in "The Story of American Business, from the Pages of The New York Times"). Back then I observed that cable-TV was a medium without a message, an industry whose chief concerns were technology and marketing.

As cable reached critical mass, its situation was strikingly similar to that of the Internet. Both were primarily delivery systems, capable of transmitting content to places where it had not been available, and in volume—"shelf space" as cable programmers termed it—that seemed almost limitless.

And just like the Internet, many of cable's early offerings were created by what are known in today's digital world as aggregators. Cable's so-called "superstations," WGN in Chicago and Ted Turner's Channel 17 in Atlanta (which later became WTBS), functioned mainly as aggregators of off-network reruns and movies. MTV was conceived to aggregate video clips that were produced as promotional pieces by record companies.

Cable's early entrepreneurs faced the same fundamental challenge that Internet operators are struggling with today: how to get consumers to pay for content that historically had been given to them for free. The cable industry solved this problem in two clever ways—by chopping the content into small pieces, and then by packaging many of those pieces together.

First, the chopping. Instead of a single channel offering news, sports, weather and entertainment, cable used its expanded shelf space to give each component its own separate channel. Back then, with the advent of CNN, ESPN, MTV, The Weather Channel, etc., the process was known as narrowcasting; today, on the Internet, it's called vertical organization of content.

On the Internet, for example, fans of classical music can subscribe to MusicalAmerica.com for $135 per year; weather buffs can stay current with the Pro package at AccuWeather.com for $250 a year. The digital choices already seem limitless—yet they're merely a hint of what's to come.

Second, the packaging. Once cable customers were hooked (literally), they were sold tiers of content, in which the narrowcast channels were combined to create simplified pricing options.

It's no accident that the first major general interest newspaper to erect a pay wall, Long Island's *Newsday*, is owned by Cablevision. By establishing a five-dollar per week "value" for Newsday.com, then packaging it with cable and Internet service, Cablevision was setting the stage for "Newsday Gold" or "Newsday Platinum" down the road—for additional fees.

Each of today's content creators—newspapers, book publishers, television, etc.—will find different lessons in cable's history. What Amazon's Kindle does with books and periodicals, what *The Wall Street Journal* does with its newspaper, and what the website Hulu.com does with TV programs, come closest to following cable's model for success in the digital world. Each has some control over both content and delivery, and each is creating multiple pricing tiers.

Based on cable's experience, it is possible that major newspapers will wind up charging for all but the most basic of online content, and it will be sold in pieces: the sports section, the opinion section, the entertainment section, and so forth. Networks of newspapers will be formed, so that for a single fee readers can access five or ten of the nation's best papers.

Perhaps the greatest lesson from TV's entrance into the video supermarket three decades ago is that cable didn't kill broadcast TV, although it forced some changes. Similarly, pay-TV didn't shut down the movie theaters.

Today, some maintain that the immediacy of the Internet and the ability of consumers to redistribute content with ease (via YouTube, for example) make earlier media models irrelevant. But the essential components of the cable revolution are likely to prevail in the digital age: content is key, and consumers will support it. Quantity is appealing, but quality sells.

And the more you look at history, the less revolutionary things become.

◆◆◆

Lowest Content Denominator

As *Newsweek* faded away and *Time* continued to struggle, each turned to greater sensationalism. While these magazines were already in media's rearview mirror, their turn toward tabloid-style reporting reflects what is happening all along the information highway.

The fuss over controversial covers began in 2011: *Time* with a 26-year-old mother breast feeding her unusually mature 3-year-old son; *Newsweek* with a rainbow halo over Barack Obama's head and the line, "America's first gay president." Selling magazines and tabloid newspapers with shock and schlock isn't new, but the fact that the techniques

have gone viral—to use new media's favorite term—is troubling.

One day's front-page headlines on AOL: "Grandma Goes to Wal-mart, Vanishes" and "I Ate to Scare Classmates Away." That same day CNN.com's top items were flesh-eating bugs and "Horse bolts into ocean, swims 2 miles." On the conservative Drudge Report: "Rocks Found at Beach Ignite in Woman's Pocket."

This is now the standard stuff of top Internet sites as well as cable-TV, broadcast TV morning shows and, of course, local TV newscasts. Even many of the most reputable news organizations, such as the *Los Angeles Times*, play it straight on their printed front pages but turn frisky online. The flesh-eating bugs and burning rocks—plus several celebrity items—were front-page news on the *Times'* website.

One major reason for this condition involves the difference between serving a stable, subscription-based audience versus non-paid, transient customers. News organizations that charge for content, especially via ongoing subscriptions, face less pressure to woo readers with the most eye-opening developments of the moment. Free media, and publications largely reliant on single-copy sales, are in a constant struggle for attention.

The most popular websites, almost all offering content for free, play the grabber game minute-to-minute, knowing that readers are just a click away from disappearing. As long as the "free model" persists in new media, the trend toward sensationalism will continue.

Another factor is the 24/7 pace of modern communication. "Breaking News" is the mantra of cable coverage—even if much of it is hardly newsworthy and is barely breaking. A truck in flames on a Midwest Interstate might qualify as breaking news on national cable—especially if there's video—but would never appear in a summary of the day's most important developments.

Then, too, there is the popularity of "reality" and celebrity-driven programming across the TV spectrum. These shows came along at just the right time to synergize with other media. Contestants perform at night and show up the next morning on competing networks to talk about it. Not since Charles Van Doren captivated the nation in 1956 on the NBC quiz program "Twenty One" have media paid so much attention to TV-created competition—and it should be remembered that Van Doren's appeal was his intellect and not, to cite a current NBC show, how much weight he could lose from one week to the next. The fact that "Twenty One" was rigged only made for better tabloid head-lines.

Tabloid topics are getting increased space, as was evidenced one day when the Huffington Post featured on its front page: "Sore Muscle Remedies that Really Work." Over on the Drudge Report, page one in-cluded: "Electronic cigarette blows up in man's face," Knife-wielding woman attacks boyfriend over Valentine's gift snub," and "Cops: Man killed in dog poop dispute."

The confounding part of this is that we're in the midst of an in-formation explosion—a virtual supermarket of news options—and Americans are stuffing themselves with sweets. Part of the explanation is that consumers have so many choices just a click away that pro-grammers don't dare bore them with seriosity. The scene at the check-out aisle, where tabloids scream for attention, is now spread across the media landscape.

A popular tool in the nation's newsrooms is an electronic tote board that provides minute-to-minute details of what's hot online. Low click counts send editors scurrying for stories or photos that will grab readers' attention.

With few exceptions, major media give consumers what they want. It's a lucky publication or broadcast that is able to find an audi-ence that actually wants meaningful news and information. Look what happened to the cable channel Bravo, launched in 1980 as a premium outlet for fine film, drama and other performing arts. Today, the chan-nel is almost entirely devoted to reality shows about real housewives, top chefs and other frivolous fare.

More "real" than any of Bravo's sappy shows is the fact that the programming represents what a vast audience now wants. But it's also our modern information systems that inspire low octane content. For example, there's a bigger audience for video than for words, which is why local TV news has long favored helicopter shots of car chases and fires. So, as news organizations build websites they tend to overdose on video clips, no matter how sugary, like those on TMZ and YouTube.

Most media, from print to radio and TV, were originally launched with meaningful approaches to information and entertainment and then, as audiences grew and competition increased, drifted more to-ward tabloidism. The Internet is experiencing this, at the accelerated pace that marks the digital world.

Sadly, increased competition among media often brings out the worst in news judgment. Consumers are blessed to have so many digital options from which to choose, and cursed that so many of them vie for attention by seeking the lowest content denominator.

While industry observers tend to view the market as divided between "paid" and "free," the distinction is also increasingly between "serious" and "superficial." There are notable exceptions, but that's the trend. Our older British cousins have long had a passion for gossipy news. If we worry about following their path socially and economically, we might as well add tabloid tendencies to the list.

I'd like to blame the media for this, but they only provide the candy. It's we who have the sweet teeth.

◆◆◆

Three I'll Miss

Three remarkably accomplished communicators passed away during a two-week period in November 2011. These three men could not have been more different in the way they functioned in their corners of the mass media world, yet each was brilliant. They touched us all, but for me there were special connections.

Tom Wicker was more than a great reporter, he was a progressive thinker who dared tread close to the line that separates impartial journalism from outright activism—at a time when it was far less common than it is today. During his three-decade career at *The New York Times* that ended in 1991, he was a powerful voice in civil rights and anti-war movements, speaking from a perch that gave him clout with presidents as well as millions of Americans.

In 1971, after writing about unacceptable prison conditions nationwide, Wicker found himself part of the story at Attica prison in upstate New York. He agreed to join a negotiating team during an uprising by inmates, and wound up watching in horror as 29 prisoners and 10 hostages died in an assault by state troopers and guards.

Wicker wrote "A Time to Die" about his experience, and many believe it was the best of his 20 books. Ten years later ABC made it into a movie. *The Times* assigned me to interview Wicker and the filmmakers to find out why the film was relatively soft while the book was so hard-hitting.

Wicker explained that, in print, "I was able to (present) a number of things involving the problems of criminal justice in America, racism and violence in America." Film, he told me, "doesn't work very well that way." Tom Wicker was a print guy all right, at a time when that was the most important thing a journalist could be.

Andy Rooney not only entertained us, he made us think—not about big, complicated matters but about little things that knit to form our lives. "Curmudgeon" was a word several writers used to describe him. Having lived a few blocks from him in Rowayton, Connecticut, I can confirm that he was as grouchy at the hardware store as he was on "60 Minutes."

What intrigued me most about Rooney was his ability to notice things in life that many of us tend to overlook, and his relentless pursuit of society's peccadilloes. Andy Rooney was the type of journalist who had the canny ability to make us think while also making us smile.

Bil Keane's work appeared in the comic section, but it managed to trigger our emotions as much as anything on the front page. "The Family Circus," a simple panel with parents and kids who haven't aged a bit

BIL KEANE · 1922-2011

since its debut in 1959, remains a staple in over 1,500 newspapers.

It's schmaltzy yet real, as when one tot asks his mother, "Can I wear my short-sleeve pants?" Or when another exclaims, "Mom's cooking my favorite dinner. It's called leftovers."

I never met Bil Keane, but often felt he was part of my family. Beginning in 1954 he drew a comic panel called "Channel Chuckles," for which one of his favorite subjects was my father's program, "Candid Camera." As always, the humor was pointed, yet kind.

Bil Keane's real-life son, Jeff, had been helping with "Family Circus" for some time, so the institution continues—a passing of the media torch with which I'm familiar.

Taken together, the work of these three men provides a good picture of what great journalism can be, regardless of the form it takes or the era in which it is practiced.

IN THE NEWS

Pricey Democracy

Most journalists love a good argument, especially when it involves their own profession. So it's not surprising that the debate over whether newspapers should charge for online content rambles on long after it has become clear that the real question is not "whether," but when? And how much?

As blueprints are drawn for online pay walls, and as newspapers implement steep price increases for their printed editions, there is a serious danger that high quality written news and analysis will become a luxury that many Americans simply can't afford. An unintended consequence of the pricing turmoil in the news business may be a nation of information haves and have-nots.

When I first wrote about this problem in a syndicated column in 2011, some editors were skeptical. They were unconvinced that papers would ever be able to put the genie back in the bottle and begin charging for Internet content—even as their own jobs were being threatened by a financial quagmire, caused in part by the decision in the early '90s to provide online material for free.

Then came a report by the Knight Foundation on the related subject of the public's access to digital information. A key finding: "In a democracy, the very idea of second-class citizenship is unacceptable; yet, for many, second-class information citizenship is looming."

In its two-year study, the Knight panel found a paradox: while digital information is expanding nationally and globally, the volume and quality of local and regional information is shrinking. The study concludes that not all Americans and their local communities are being served equally in the digital world.

When the Knight data are layered against shifts in the newspaper industry, the situation becomes more clear but no less troubling. The vast majority of daily papers serve small and medium-sized communities. When they cut staff and pages the result is usually less local coverage. Although several notable attempts have been made to replace this lost information with local Internet news—such as the short-lived online version of Denver's defunct *Rocky Mountain News*—far more coverage is disappearing each year than is being replaced in the digital arena.

Remember, too, that even "free" Internet content comes at a significant price for the consumer. Even before the pay walls go up at major news sites, the cost of owning a computer and connecting to the Internet is fairly substantial.

Almost every analysis of the plight facing newspapers and news magazines includes the prediction that some will disappear while the survivors will have to charge substantially higher prices for their product—both in print and online. Before folding its print edition, *Newsweek* tried a business model based upon a sharply reduced circulation base of elite readers who would theoretically have been willing to pay a higher price per copy.

Where does that leave people without Internet access who simply are not able to afford print editions? *The New York Times* is at $2.50 and *The Wall Street Journal* $2. Meanwhile, some 20 percent of American adults don't have access to the Internet, and about 12 percent are without either cable or satellite TV.

Those who scoff that many low-wage earners don't care to buy *The Times* or *The Journal*—or, for that matter, access the Internet—are missing the bigger point. The nation has already suffered a severe erosion of its middle class. One way to ensure that the lower classes stay put is to allow the gulf to widen between those with easy access to information and those for whom it is unaffordable.

And those who counter that "news" can be found for free in video and audio formats need only be reminded that cable and radio have been largely taken over by ranting purveyors of disinformation, while in many markets "your late local news" on broadcast TV consists of little more than car crashes and burning buildings. It's free, but it's hardly a replacement for well-reported news on important subjects.

In summing up its analysis of the information gap, the Knight study warns, "How we react, individually and collectively, to this democratic shortfall will affect the quality of our lives and the very nature of our communities."

Saving the newspaper industry will take some doing. Preserving the ability of all citizens to afford quality news will require even more.

Big Media's Latest Mistake

Here's a bold strategy to help struggling big league sports teams: ask the community to contribute players. For instance, instead of using only highly paid pros on the baseball diamond, try adding a citizen shortstop. And how about enlisting bloggers to serve as coaches?

OK, you're right. Such desperate measures would eventually ruin teams, and before long fans would stop paying to come to games since they can always watch low-caliber competition for free in the backyard.

Yet this is exactly where many of the nation's struggling news organizations—particularly newspapers—are headed, in what is shaping up to be the second-biggest media miscalculation since the rise of the Internet.

The first, beginning in the mid-1990s, was publishing the same content for free on the Internet that readers were asked to pay for in print. The second, now taking hold, is trying to compete with social, interactive media by mimicking their techniques. The public is being encouraged to both play and pay.

The oxymoron "citizen journalist" is turning up not only at newspapers but also at TV and radio stations as well as on the Internet. The sports analogy fits because unlike professions such as law and medicine, for which formal training is an accepted necessity, journalism and sports are attempted at all skill levels. Many amateurs believe they could hit like Albert Pujols or report like Carl Bernstein—if only given the chance.

There's nothing wrong with encouraging input from the community, which is why most papers have a letters section. There's also room for, say, an amateur's photo if he and his cellphone happen to be at the right spot when news occurs.

This is not to downgrade the importance of amateur writers and videographers, whose efforts via social media have had significant impact—most notably during political protests in the Middle East and at the Occupy movements across the United States. But the notion that mainstream—if that's the term that fits—news organizations can morph into communal information exchanges and still maintain journalistic and business viability is a bad bet.

One example is what's loosely referred to as "coffee shop journalism." Strange as it sounds, quite a few papers are closing regional bureaus and instructing the displaced professional reporters to camp in coffee shops to get a sense of what the caffeine-conscious citizenry thinks is newsworthy. Some publications are setting up storefront workstations and inviting the public in to chat about community news.

MediaNews's large Bay Area News Group, covering the San Francisco region, is opening "community news labs" at several of its papers. The group president, Mac Tully, said the goal is to "listen, engage, learn and share." According to Tully, "This strategy is in the forefront of the newspaper industry's transition from print-centric businesses to locally focused providers of news and information across multiple platforms."

Coffee shop journalism is a result of budget cutbacks and confusion among publishers about their role in the digital marketplace. While several large publications—such as *The Wall Street Journal* and *The New York Times*—have found that online revenue is not as difficult to generate as was once feared, numerous smaller papers are less certain about what readers will support in electronic formats.

At many small and mid-sized papers, community volunteers submit stories, unpaid interns file reports, and the printed newspaper page summarizes Internet blogs. Worse, the copy-desk function is being cut back or eliminated, so the writing of under trained contributors isn't even getting the scrutiny formerly provided to the veteran staffers. That's not journalism, nor is it much of a business strategy.

Mr. Tully is quite right that "locally focused" reporting is key. The way to expand and improve such coverage is to hire more trained journalists and give them adequate time for enterprise reporting—not to sell off desks and send reporters to coffee shops in search of local gossip.

News organizations can use all the citizens they can get—in the bleachers, not on the field of play.

◆◆◆

CONSUMERS ARE IN THIS TOGETHER

Money Squawks

Everyone has a story about getting ripped off by an airline, abused by the phone company, or hosed at the department of motor vehicles. And ever since the economy turned sour, we've all got grim tales to share about being beaten up by banks and credit card companies. Here are two of mine:

My Chase Visa payment was due on the Fourth of July. As a patriotic gesture I took the day off to celebrate our independence and assumed that Chase was doing the same. I paid my bill in full, electronically, on the morning of July 5.

On my next bill, Chase Visa charged me a $25 "late fee" plus $33.90 interest.

Only after eight minutes of recorded messages and music, 10 minutes with an arrogant agent, and six or seven minutes with her supervisor, was I able to get the charges removed. But that came with a stern lecture from the supervisor about how late payments would not be tolerated in the future—I assume she meant on Thanksgiving Day—and that only because of my good payment history was she able to reverse the charges.

A few months earlier I went to pay my MasterCard bill and saw that I owed a total of 17 cents. Misguidedly clinging to some old rule about "sums under one dollar," I decided to let it wait until it was time to pay the following month. For this I was charged a "late fee" of $25.

The National Credit Card Act was supposed to help combat this, capping late fees at $25 for the first offense, and $35 for the second slip within a six-month period. The law also requires fees and penalties to be "reasonable and proportional" to the violation.

One particular provision caught my eye: If due dates fall on weekends or holidays, payments must be credited to the account on the next business day without penalties. So why didn't the law protect me on July 4th? It turns out that if I had made my electronic payment on the 4th it would have been credited on the 5th with no fee; however, by making it on the morning of the 5th I was legally "late" because I failed to initiate it on the holiday. Leave it to bankers to find this loop-hole.

Americans currently hold an estimated 610 million credit cards, and each month a relatively small percent of them are not paid on time. As a result, credit card companies collect nearly $30 billion in late fees each year. It's a business on top of a business—similar to the way airlines now make exorbitant profits from itinerary change fees, baggage fees, etc.

Meanwhile, banks are squeezing consumers as never before, with new fees for checking accounts, and virtually no interest on savings.

This month, many banks cut rates on four- and five-year certifi-cates of deposit to historic lows.

Still, we small potatoes couldn't help but laugh at the announce-ment by Bank of New York Mellon Corp. when it decided to charge cus-tomers a fee if they deposit *too much* money. Under the program, any client depositing more than $50 million is required to pay the bank a penalty.

It's worth noting that Bank of New York Mellon currently has over $26 trillion in its custody.

Meanwhile, as I fretted over my two frustrating experiences with bank credit cards, I wondered if it's really true that everyone has at least one complaint. So I asked my barber, Rick, if he has a banking beef.

"Are you kidding?" he replied. He ran into the back room and came back with his monthly bank statement from Chase.

"I've got almost two thousand dollars in there," said Rick. "And look at this line, right here where it gives the total monthly interest they paid. How much did I get? One penny."

Chase is lucky it didn't offer Rick that interest for his thoughts.

◆◆◆

Clubbed

It was Groucho Marx who famously stated, "I would never belong to any club that would have me as a member."

Smart guy. If he were still around today Groucho would never find himself at the checkout counter fumbling through dozens of club cards. Of course for his obstinence he'd have to pay exorbitant prices, and most other shoppers would figure he was nuts.

Personally, I haven't enjoyed being in a club since Cub Scouts. Yet, I'm in the Sandwich Club (at my local store you buy five and the sixth sandwich is free); I'm in the Yogurt Club (where the 11th is free); I also belong to the Wellness Club at the pharmacy, the Rewards Club at the bookstore, plus the Video Club and the Carwash Club to name just a few. When I travel I try to always stay at the hotel that honors my Gold Club Membership. And day in and day out there's the biggest fraternity of all: the Supermarket Club.

A company in Cincinnati that keeps track of these things says American consumers hold 2.1 billion memberships in retail clubs, or "loyalty programs" as the industry terms them. That works out to about 18 memberships per household.

And what are consumers getting for all this besides a bulge in the wallet, as more cards squeeze in where the cash used to be? Not many bargains, that's for sure. It's been pretty well documented that virtually all retailers offering discounts to club members have jacked up prices so that members wind up paying about the same as they would at a store that didn't have a club.

The primary benefit to retailers is that clubs allow them to gather data about customers' habits and preferences. This information is valuable in designing the next round of promotions and sales, as well as targeting e-mail offerings to club members based on their purchasing history.

Then there's the "loyalty" piece, which presumably draws consumers to stores to which they "belong." Trouble is, with over 2 billion memberships out there, many consumers now have cards for every shopping occasion. How much loyalty can, say, each of the three pharmacies in a town expect if shoppers carry cards from all three stores?

Rite Aid, which has a Wellness Club, enrolled 29 million members in the first eight months, and the number has soared to over 45 million. To promote loyalty, Rite Aid offers levels of membership—Bronze, Silver and Gold—with rewards growing at each plateau.

As the *Los Angeles Times* put it, the goal of all such clubs is "to cater to the deal addiction of cash-strapped customers."

Like South American countries that balance the books by revaluing their currency, many merchants are upping their club deals by selling admission to higher levels of membership. At Barnes & Noble, for example, being a "member" costs $25 a year and provides better discounts and other perks. GameStop has a free club, but also sells membership in its Power Up Pro section for $14.99.

These schemes may be intended to make elite members feel special, but the actual effect seems to be that regular shoppers feel left out and ripped off.

Supermarket News magazine quoted a store owner in Bend, Ore., Rudy Dory, who actually said, presumably with a straight face, that his program is designed so that employees can identify club members and treat them with "extra friendliness and consideration."

That really gets to the heart of why Groucho would have hated shopping clubs. Here's a final thought from the comedian who, it seems, was quite the prescient shopper: "I have a mind to join a club and beat you over the head with it."

◆ ◆ ◆

Patriotic Purchasing

Is it unpatriotic for Americans to buy foreign-made products? President Obama once declared, "I'm convinced we're going to rebuild [the economy] better and stronger than before. And at its heart is going to be three powerful words: Made in America."

You'd think that would be a call to action—for government to encourage domestic manufacturing, and for consumers to aggressively support it.

Yet, at a time when many Americans are easily agitated about immigrants crossing our borders, they seem to care little about the flood of foreign-made products. While they decry the loss of jobs and the flight of manufacturing to cheaper locales overseas, most consumers remain oblivious to distinctions concerning where products are made and by whom.

"You see a whole bunch of Korean cars here in the United States," President Obama noted, "and you don't see any American cars in Korea." That's a slight oversimplification, but only slight.

According to the U.S. Commerce Department, for every U.S.-made car exported to Korea, 30 Korean-made cars are exported to the U.S. (this does not count Korean models assembled in the U.S.) In all, roughly half the cars Americans buy each year are manufactured by foreign-owned companies.

No reasonable person would advocate slashing the tires of every Hyundai parked on their block, but why isn't owning a foreign car more stigmatized? Remember back in 2003 when some Americans had snit fits about France's reluctance to support our military effort in Iraq? It prompted a boycott of "French fries," even though the French have nothing to do with our fries.

Many Americans passionately object to telephone "customer service" agents who sound suspiciously as if they're speaking from offshore—in the Philippines, perhaps—but those same consumers drive Korean-made cars without giving it much of a thought.

Is that consumer ambivalence or ignorance?

Part of the problem for well-intentioned Americans when it comes to buying foreign cars—or, for that matter, foreign-made TV sets, computers and numerous other high-ticket items—is that the information about where things are produced is fuzzy. Some Fords, for example, are built in Mexico, using designs created in Japan. At the same time, Hyundai is increasing its production here in the U.S.

Even many iconic American products aren't made here anymore. Barbie, perhaps America's most famous doll, is made by Mattel in China. Levi's jeans are all made overseas. Rawlings, the exclusive supplier of Major League baseballs, manufacturers every single ball in Costa Rica. Laptops, cellphones, television sets, and even light bulbs—none is made in the U.S.

In fact, it's virtually impossible to buy exclusively American these days, although the situation is shifting slightly. The cost of foreign labor is inching up, while shipping costs from overseas have climbed.

According to *Fortune* magazine, Illinois-based Caterpillar, the world's largest maker of excavators and bulldozers, relocated some of its excavator production from abroad to Texas. U.S. furniture maker Sauder moved production back home from low-wage countries.

Not surprisingly, domestic entrepreneurs are seeking to cash in on the desire of some Americans to buy U.S.-made products. The All American Clothing Co. in Ohio, for example, boasts that its products are made entirely in America by Americans, using American-made materials. There are numerous websites, such as Made Here In America, and I Buy US Made, dedicated to identifying American products.

Apple slyly labels its products as "designed in California," although most are still made in China.

Not too long ago it would have been viewed as xenophobic for Americans to boycott goods simply because they were made in other countries. Now, along with other elements related to our troubled economy, that's changed.

Ponder this from Moody's Economy.com: If every American spent an extra six cents a week on U.S.-made products, it would create nearly 10,000 new jobs a year.

◆◆◆

Customer Service Travels Well

Each year as Labor Day approaches and vacation season draws to a close, many Americans are so stressed by the rigors of travel that they're happy to have a vacation from vacations.

Anyone who's taken a plane ride recently knows how unpleasant the process has become. Although most airlines are reporting an upswing in passenger volume, customer service seems to have reached a record low.

The nation's hotel chains, which took a similar beating when the economy tanked, are also seeing modest improvement in occupancy. But here's the twist: customer service—particularly among mid-priced hotels—is soaring and may be nearing an all-time high.

Why are these two cornerstones of the travel business so diametrically different when it comes to pleasing customers? How is it that most hotel chains are battling to gain customers by serving them well, while major airlines seem audacious enough to seek passengers while treating them poorly?

Most of my flying is on United Airlines, simply because it dominates the routes out of the small airport near my home in Central California. I'm often compelled to fly United despite its customer service, not because of it.

On the road, I've become a big fan of Hilton's Hampton Inn brand, not because of limited choices, but because I'm so impressed by the level of service and value I've experienced at many of Hampton's 1,700 locations. The customer service dynamic is dramatically different between these two areas of the travel world.

For a clear example of how the industries have diverged, look no further than the "points" or "mileage" award programs. The concept of earning free service by collecting points was invented by airlines roughly 30 years ago. Today, the airline programs are a mess, with trillions of unused miles and great frustration among fliers who accumulate points and then find how increasingly difficult it is to use them.

The Hilton Honors system on the other hand is simple, convenient and, best of all, it works. With very few exceptions, the hotel industry has not crippled its award programs with too many blackout dates or other restrictions. As a result, the programs foster consumer loyalty for all the right reasons.

Another profound example is in ticky-tack charges. Airlines seem sold on the notion that charging separate fees for everything from luggage to pillows to boarding priority results in greater revenue, which earnings reports indicate it has. But at what expense? Most fliers are fuming.

I bought a round-trip ticket for my son on US Airways, going from Washington, D.C., to Monterey, Calif., with a change of planes in Phoenix. Just before the trip I learned I had business that required me to be in the Phoenix area, so I met him there and we drove home to Monterey. The following week, when he tried to make the return trip from Monterey to Washington, the airline said we owed a $150 "change fee." What change? US Airways claimed it was that Danny declined to use the Phoenix-Monterey portion of his ticket.

Contrast that with the sign posted at each Hampton Inn advising that if you're unhappy with any aspect of service, your stay is free. A survey by J.D. Power and Associates showed increased satisfaction among North American hotel guests in every category measured.

The top five hotel perks according to the survey are: free Internet, free breakfast, choice of bedding, pillow-top mattresses and free parking. Hampton Inn, like most of its mid-priced competitors, offers all these and more. Newspapers, toothpaste, coffee 24/7, a brown-bag snack for your journey—it's all included in the basic rate.

J.D. Power also reported a slight increase in satisfaction among airline passengers in the first half of 2010, but except for perennial standout Alaska Airlines, the uptick seemed to reflect surrender by consumers rather than a vote of approval. It may be marginally less annoying to ride a plane these days, but nearly half of passengers surveyed said that prices for in-flight beverages and food, checked baggage, and preferred seating are unreasonably high.

Consolidation of airlines has left fliers with little leverage. Other factors impacting air travel, from security to yo-yoing fuel prices, make it tough on carriers as well as their passengers. But there is something fundamentally wrong with the airlines' approach to customer service—and it's vividly clear when compared with the strides taken by hotel chains.

Someone once said, "getting there is half the fun," but nowadays the travel industry is changing the equation.

Branded

While taking a shower at the Hampton Inn in Franklin, Mass., I noticed some information printed on the tiny bottle of shampoo. On one side it said "shampoo," which I found to be both appropriate and useful. On the other side it said "www.hampton.com," a notation that was baffling under the circumstances.

As I rinsed off it dawned on me that had I thought to bring my iPad into the shower I could have sent management an e-mail: "pls deliver 2 btowels to rm 320 asap :)"

Apparently one significant aspect of the Internet Revolution is that businesses now believe it is essential to, as marketing people term it, "brand" their URL addresses in as many crannies as possible. Some firms, it seems, would rather be known as a website address than as, say, an actual company.

Looking around my hotel room I discovered the address—that's hampton.com—emblazoned on the bottle of conditioner, the moisturizer, the mouthwash, the plastic drinking cup, the laundry bag, the room key, the ballpoint pen, and even on each sheet of paper on the notepad I used to make this list. That's either what you call high-powered website branding, or Internet Era overkill.

Meanwhile, it's come to my attention that eight states now print their website addresses on license plates. If you're driving behind someone in Florida, Pennsylvania, Georgia, Michigan, Maryland, Nebraska, South Carolina or Minnesota, you'll know instantly how to reach state government via the Internet with a message such as, "There's a dead squirrel at Mile 147 of I-95."

I doubt state legislators wish to encourage motorists to use the Internet while driving, so what exactly is the purpose of stamping the addresses on license plates? Did a highly paid marketing person actually sit in a room and say, "I'll bet more people would shop here in Nebraska if only we had our URL address on license plates"?

Flying on United Airlines I noticed that United.com is printed in large type on every paper napkin. Here again, I must be missing the big point. You've already managed to contact the airline in order to buy your ticket, so is the idea that you'll stick the dirty napkin in your bag and carry it around in case someday, after you've forgotten how to contact United Airlines, you'll refer to the napkin and be reminded of United.com?

A byproduct of this online obsession is the fact that many companies simply don't want customers calling them on the phone—never, ever, for any reason, anymore, period. Most banks and airlines are already there. They hide their phone numbers more artfully than Hollywood celebrities. And if you somehow track down a number, you run the risk of paying a penalty for daring to use the phone. You're also in for a tedious button-pushing ordeal to get through the screening system, ending with an automated: "Thanks, I'll be sure to pass that information to an agent."

The agent, who is likely to be housed in an unidentified offshore location, has a strange way of speaking English which is eerily robotic in tone and execution. Regardless, he or she has not been given any of the information that you punched in, and is usually of so little help that you'll be trained never to bypass the Internet again, ever.

One regional carrier, Allegiant Air, now makes it impossible to phone them without a charge, stating on their website: "...we have chosen to reduce our costs by discontinuing our toll-free number." If you do choose to phone the 702 area code, you'll find that there is a $10 fee per passenger, per segment flown, for using the "Call Center." So it's worth a lot of money if you can find a paper napkin that might have Allegiant's URL on it.

Bottom line: I think we may all be overdoing the website thing just a tad. I'd also like to mention that readers will find an extensive collection of our entertaining DVDs and other great merchandise at www.CandidCamera.com.

◆◆◆

Rx for Confusion

For many years I've been taking a prescription arthritis drug with which, according to an ominous sounding voice on television, "serious, sometimes fatal events have occurred."

Speaking as one who is not a medical professional, I concur that death qualifies as a serious event. Then again, my doctor has assured me that few people actually suffer this event, or most of the numerous other events rattled off by the TV announcer.

The drug, known as Enbrel, definitely succeeds in making me feel better. But the television commercial, shown with alarming regularity, is enough to make me sick.

The U.S. and New Zealand are the only nations to allow consumer-directed advertising of prescription drugs. The door in the U.S. was opened in 1997 when the FDA relaxed its ad policies, leading to what is now $5 billion in annual spending by drug companies seeking to influence consumers to in turn influence their doctors to prescribe specific drugs.

The head of the American Medical Association, Dr. Nancy Nielson, told Congress that most AMA members are against direct-to-consumer ads. Such ads, she said, "often portray drugs through rose-colored glasses by including more information about a drug's benefits than risks."

On the other hand, you'd need a rose-colored hearing aid to ignore the TV warnings about side effects—ranging from the common (dizziness, drowsiness and nausea), to the unusual (compulsive gambling and suicide), to the one that seems to have garnered the most attention (erections lasting more than four hours).

There is little reason to allow consumer ads for prescription drugs other than to protect a $5 billion marketing business. And now that the pharmaceutical industry has agreed to stop giving doctors free pens, mugs, T-shirts and other promotional tchotchkes, enlisting patients to lobby on behalf of advertised drugs is more valuable than ever.

Virtually all American adults (91%) indicate having seen prescription drug ads, and 32% of them say they asked their doctor about a specific drug they saw advertised, according to a study by the Harvard School of Public Health. Among those who spoke to their doctor about an advertised medicine, 44% percent say they were given a prescription for that drug.

Critics argue that such doctor-patient exchanges waste time and encourage the use of costly and possibly unnecessary medications.

Moreover, relentless warnings on television are frighteningly lacking in context, and may be counterproductive. A serious side-effect could be to dissuade patients from taking treatments for which their doctors believe the benefits outweigh the risks.

The FDA requires that TV ads for prescription drugs include "a fair balance between information about effectiveness and information about risk." The major risks are to be covered in "consumer-friendly language."

Madison Avenue's response to these regulations frequently involves video scenes of "effectiveness"—such as a patient with arthritis playing the piano—coupled with audio covering "risks" such as death. This is a prescription for confusion.

Research by Duke University found that 80% of viewers can recall benefits of drugs promoted in commercials, but only 20% successfully remember the stated risks. A UCLA study suggests that TV ads may be influencing viewers to believe they are sicker than they really are, and this could lead to taking medicine in excess.

While pouring money into consumer advertising, the drug industry continues to bend to public pressure by expanding its list of voluntary guidelines. Beginning in 2009, guidelines stated that viewers should be informed when actors portray doctors; that ads featuring real doctors should disclose that they have been paid; and that celebrity endorsements should reflect the individuals' actual opinions about the drug.

But The Pharmaceutical Research and Manufacturers of America refused to include one guideline requested by several members of Congress, that companies wait until drugs have been on the market for two years before advertising them directly to consumers.

The FDA went so far as to ask Congress for permission to produce a fake commercial for blood pressure medicine, to measure to what extent the warning statements were getting through. I imagine the results of such research would underscore the problem with most ads for prescription drugs: some viewers become overly worried by ominous warnings, while others are oblivious and don't focus on the warnings at all.

Sixty-second commercials are not suitable forums for presenting the weights and measures of complex medical issues. Although an unrestricted flow of information is always desirable for the public good, a barrage of ads promoting confusion and fear is certainly not healthful.

LIFE AND TAXES

Voluntary Tax Break

Seems there are almost as many theories about how to change the tax laws as there are citizens to whom the laws apply. Here's one simple idea—a modest proposal that would help Americans at all income levels pay a bit less, while also providing some benefit to the unemployed.

Give the nation's nonpaid volunteers a tax credit for their service.

Unlike charity in the form of money and goods, the truly benevolent volunteer efforts by Americans who donate their time is not acknowledged by the IRS. I'm speaking of volunteers who receive no compensation whatsoever, as opposed to paid volunteers such as those who serve in the military.

According to The Bureau of Labor Statistics, volunteering among Americans climbed in 2010 and 2011, then dropped slightly in 2012. This suggests that volunteering tends to follow patterns of economic hardship and unemployment, as more citizens respond to the need to pitch in.

Roughly 64 million people volunteer for charitable causes in the U.S. each year, at the rate of about an hour per week. Almost all of this donated sweat—delivering meals to the poor, coaching youth sports teams, etc.—is targeted at fundamental human needs, yet none of it is tax deductible.

Ironically, the IRS allows volunteers to deduct the cost of transportation to their nonpaying jobs, but not the value of the work itself. How could this value be computed?

The average hourly wage for all civilian American employees, excluding farm workers, stands at $23.82 at this writing. A reasonable formula would take 25 percent of this figure, $5.96, as the allowable per-hour tax deduction for documented volunteering.

Volunteer workers should be allowed to carry the credits forward for, say, five years. This would allow unemployed volunteers to benefit in the future, while inspiring them to make productive use of their available time in the present.

Yes, participating organizations would have to qualify as non-profits, just as they must to receive tax-deductible cash donations. Yes, charities would have to provide written records for workers, which is what they already do for monetary donors. And, to be certain, there would be abuses. But whom should the IRS worry about more: the billionaire who bends the rules when claiming a five-digit deduction, or the Meals on Wheels driver who adds 15 minutes to his time sheet?

Granting a tax deduction for volunteer service would be a step toward correcting serious inequities among paid and unpaid workers performing the same functions. For example, many U.S. communities have the means to employ fulltime fire fighters, while other locales rely on strictly volunteer forces. Why shouldn't the volunteers be entitled to a tax deduction? Hospital workers, school employees and other professionals often work side-by-side with unpaid volunteers who deserve a tax break for their service.

Based on current levels of volunteerism, the cost of such a deduction would be about $850 million per year if used completely by all who are eligible. More likely, some volunteers would not take the deduction, while others would be motivated to add volunteer hours, leaving the price tag under $1 billion annually.

At a time when tax-deductible monetary donations in the U.S. are falling—to roughly $303 billion—and unemployment remains unacceptably high, it's logical to inspire and compensate volunteers for their service.

Presidents have long advocated volunteerism, from John Kennedy's "ask not what your country can do for you," to George H. W. Bush's "a thousand points of light," to George W. Bush's "new culture of responsibility." As Barack Obama put it, "The need for action always exceeds the limits of government."

Most nonpaid servants give their time without any thought whatsoever of receiving anything in return. And that's precisely why acknowledging them with a modest tax reward makes perfect sense.

◆◆◆

Lotteries are Losers

The precocious talking baby in E-Trade commercials offers sage advice about state-run lotteries: "Your chances of winning," he tells a delusional adult friend, "are the same as the odds of you being mauled by a polar bear and a regular bear on the same day."

I thought of that one evening as I watched the long line of sad souls at a 7-Eleven store in the older, less affluent West Side of Alexandria, Va., waiting patiently to kiss their money goodbye on the lottery. It stuck in my mind because the previous day I saw an almost identical scene at a variety store on a rundown stretch of Route 59 in Nanuet, N.Y.

In Maryland, the newspaper I picked up said the state was about to begin selling lottery tickets on the Internet. Driving up and down the Northeast corridor, I heard incessant lottery commercials like the one in New York that promised "Tahitian sunsets," and another that claimed with a big win you could finally "be your own boss."

There's nothing new—or, in my opinion, good—about lotteries. But these days, with many state governments strapped, and so many of their residents hurting, it's a perfect storm.

The arguments haven't changed much since New Hampshire became the first state to run a lottery back in 1964. The view among supporters is that people will gamble if they want, so government might as well reap the profits. Besides, the money goes to good causes, usually education, which would otherwise require funding through higher taxes.

Currently, 43 states run lotteries, with annual wagers totaling about $55 billion.

I've never been keen on lotteries. The odds of winning are worse than virtually any bet you could make in a casino. But on a more fundamental basis, I don't think government should be in the gambling business. Moreover, state-created advertising for lotteries is shameful—preying on the vulnerabilities of those desperate for a financial fix. New York State spends roughly $50 million every year on ads to lure people into the game.

Online lottery sales, launched this year in Illinois, raise the stakes on this dubious government gambit. Interestingly, the primary op-

position to Internet lottery sales comes not from concerned citizens, but from retailers who fear that electronic marketing will cut into in-store business.

After Illinois, Georgia approved online sales, and several more states are rushing to embrace it with the fervor of addicted gamblers. It's possible because the U.S. Justice Department last year reversed itself, saying the national Wire Act of 1961 applies only to sports betting.

Georgia is the worst "sucker state" for lottery players, according to Bloomberg News, which weighed pay-offs against odds as well as average state income. Georgia even has its own debit card cunningly named iHope, which can be used for both in-store and online lottery purchases.

Several studies confirm that state lottery revenue comes disproportionately from lower-income residents. Lotteries allow governments to take advantage of the very citizens they should be striving to protect.

It's too late to put this genie back in the bottle. States will never give up lottery revenue—certainly not in these crushing economic times. But responsible legislators should proceed with caution when it comes to online sales.

In 2012, Delaware became the first state to authorize online casino-style gambling. "If you stand still, you'll lose ground," Delaware's lottery director, Vernon Kirk, told the Wall Street Journal. He's referring to the fact that although lottery revenue is growing in most states, the number of new players is not. Kirk and other bureaucrats see the Internet as a tool for attracting customers who have never purchased a lottery ticket in a store.

Lottery commercials all end with a wink and the throwaway line: "Play responsibly." State legislators probably don't listen to their own ads, and they're hoping their customers don't either.

Taxes Make Dull Tools

If you don't drink soda, it's of little concern that taxes are being proposed to limit consumption of sugary drinks, just as those of us who are nonsmokers don't give much thought to punitive taxes aimed at discouraging tobacco use.

Yet, the question raised by these and a raft of socially-targeted taxes is whether they unfairly discriminate against people who don't happen to have a lot of money. Put another way: Is it reasonable for government to try to alter behavior by placing a price on it?

In Massachusetts, the debate centered on a proposed tax for soda and candy that would have brought the state as much as $50 million a year. The tax wouldn't be new, the argument went, since the proposal involved removing the exemption on certain sweets rather than applying a new and targeted tax.

In nearby New York State there was excitement in some quarters about the prospect of "raising $222 million a year" (that was the headline), by imposing a half-cent per ounce tax uniquely aimed at curbing consumption of soda.

Who exactly would be discouraged by having to spend a few pennies more for soda pop? Certainly not rich folks. Why would anyone willing to pay, say, $12 for glass of fairly mundane merlot at the bar, think twice about spending a penny more for a can of Pepsi at the convenience store?

Punitive taxes can only modify the behavior of those for whom the tax is truly punitive.

Historically, "sin taxes"—primarily on tobacco, alcohol and gambling—were implemented to cash in on socially risky behavior rather than to curb it. The U.S. has taxed cigarettes since the Civil War but only in recent years, with the federal tax climbing above a dollar a pack, has it been viewed as a serious attempt to discourage consumption. Even then, does anyone truly believe that if President Obama succeeds in kicking his cigarette habit it will be due in any way whatsoever to the tax on a pack?

In California, an example of how twisted things can become when government tries to affect both behavior and revenue is seen in the handling of highway carpool lanes, sometimes called High Occupancy Vehicle lanes. The original premise was both wise and democratic: encourage motorists to reduce congestion and pollution by sharing rides, and reward them with their own speedy lane. But then, lawmakers eager to raise money began amending the rules for HOV lanes by opening them to unaccompanied motorists willing to pay a fee.

The practical effect is that the state will make money, the average motorist without a companion and unable to afford the tariff will take longer to get to work, and the Ferraris will fly by solo.

It's said that the Massachusetts soda tax would have been used to support health care programs, while also discouraging consumption of drinks that contribute to obesity. That's a zero-sum proposition. If the tax actually succeeds in reducing soda sales, the revenue will dwindle as well.

In all likelihood a few cents in taxes won't significantly affect either sales or obesity. It will provide the state with additional revenue, and it will create another small hardship for those least able to afford it.

If government really wants to promote healthy behavior, conserve water, reduce pollution, or promote other good causes, it should create the necessary programs and provide the proper incentives. On the other hand, if government needs money, it should collect it without dubious pretense.

◆ ◆ ◆

HOME WORK

Do It Yourself (Poorly)

There was a time, not too long ago, when "do-it-yourself" meant trying to fix the leaky shower head without the help of a professional plumber. Or changing the oil in your car without a mechanic.

Nowadays it means much more. Technology and enhanced communication have ushered in an era with numerous opportunities to do it yourself—and, for many practitioners, to do it poorly.

My own career has centered on two fields now overrun with do-it-yourselfism: television and journalism. TV used to be a big, expensive process, left mostly to trained professionals. Then everyone's Uncle Harry got a camcorder. Now, with little more than a cell phone and access to YouTube, we're all television producers.

Journalism? There's hardly a more explosive do-it-yourself field than the Fourth Estate. The line between citizen journalists and their professional counterparts is increasingly blurred—or blogged. According to the website BlogPulse, roughly 65,000 new blogs are created every day, with the total number of blogs estimated at 183 million as of early 2013 when BlogPulse apparently choked on its numbers and went out of business.

But thanks to the Internet we now also have do-it-yourself lawyering, accounting and, of course, stock brokering. All this isn't necessarily bad: Some professions were rightly doomed as technology gave consumers the tools to do things faster and cheaper on their own. The travel agency business comes to mind.

So are we now returning to an era of self-sufficiency? Or is this the dawn of an age of do-it-yourself mediocrity?

On the popular WebMD website, there is an article titled, "Do-It-Yourself Dentistry." Included is this bit of instruction for replacing your own crown or cap: "Clean it out thoroughly, and either buy paste in a drugstore or mix your own with Vaseline and corn starch. Mix it to be a pretty thick paste. Then, put the paste in the crown, place it on the tooth, and bite down gently until it's seated. Wipe off extra glue that will seep out."

Marriage on the rocks? "It used to be hard to get a do-it-yourself divorce, but not anymore," states the website Do-It-Yourself-Service.com.

Problems with your immigration status? Websites such as usavisanow.com offer products like "The Complete Do-It-Yourself Immigration Kit."

Yet rather than eliminating jobs, perhaps our determination to do things ourselves is creating an even larger need for professionals to clean up after us—much as the circus discovered the need for workers to follow behind the elephants.

My doctor complains that he must now spend an inordinate amount of time with many patients, trying to correct snippets of half-truths and misdiagnoses that they've acquired from do-it-yourself on-line doctoring.

The real problem with, say, do-it-yourself wedding photography is that the photos look like they were taken with Aunt Julia's cellphone, because they were. We teach ourselves Spanish on the Internet and then wonder why we can't even order a taco.

Personally, my attempt to repair the shower head only resulted in a small flood in the bathroom, water damage to the room below, and eventually a call to a plumber who did his best to avoid snickering while fixing the thing.

Daydream Believer

This is a dream come true. Researchers at Carnegie Mellon University sity have made a scientific discovery that should thrill those who are overweight but spend much time picturing their next meal.

The better you are at conjuring up images of yourself munching food, the less likely you are to actually overeat.

Who knew?

"These findings suggest that trying to suppress one's thoughts of desired foods in order to curb cravings for those foods is a fundamentally flawed strategy," said Carey Morewedge, author of the report.

"Our studies found that instead, people who repeatedly imagined the consumption of a morsel of food—such as an M&M or cube of cheese—subsequently consumed less of that food than did people who imagined consuming the food a few times or performed a different but similarly engaging task."

Not since Professor Harold Hill discovered that students could master playing band instruments by using the Think System in "The Music Man," has there been such hope for daydream believers.

"We think these findings will help develop future interventions to reduce cravings for things such as unhealthy food, drugs and cigarettes," said Morewedge.

The key to the discovery involves a process known as "habituation," by which imagining an experience becomes a substitute for really doing it. Thus, in order to reduce their actual intake, participants in the study had to imagine themselves consuming food rather than simply picturing the food itself. With M&M candies, researchers said imagining yourself eating 30 of them, one at a time, would likely result in you eating less when you turned to the real thing.

How far can this go? Can we imagine our way to a thicker head of hair? Is there benefit to envisioning more digits on our paychecks?

Skeptics will point out that for over 100 years baseball fans in Chicago have pictured the Cubs winning the World Series, but it hasn't brought them a championship. Then there's the fact that the world did not come to an end despite the prediction and vivid imagination of California preacher Harold Camping.

On the other hand, we all know that Rep. John Boehner devoted many months to picturing himself as Speaker of the House and then miraculously attained the position. Ann Curry spent 14 years at the "Today" show picturing herself in the anchor seat, and finally got the job only to lose it a short time later. And what does habituation tell us about the future for Sarah Palin, who seems to have conjured detailed mental images of herself in the White House—right down to what she'll be wearing at cabinet meetings?

In the words of Eleanor Roosevelt, "The future belongs to those who believe in the beauty of their dreams."

Right now in my dreams I'm picturing myself on a beach, looking more fit than ever before, sipping a cocktail from a glass with one of those paper umbrellas in it, tapping out a Pulitzer Prize-winning column on a laptop given to me along with a personal tutorial by Apple's Tim Cook, while Barack Obama waits patiently to ask my advice about something as soon as Lady Gaga finishes just one more song.

Of course, I'm counting on the fact that Prof. Morewedge and his colleagues at Carnegie Mellon actually conducted their research, rather than just sitting around imagining it.

◆ ◆ ◆

KIDS AND THE LAW

Juvenile Injustice

Many of the nation's prosecutors and judges continue to put kids on trial as adults. This, despite declining crime rates among juveniles and growing scientific evidence about the inappropriateness of taking young offenders out of the court system designed specifically to protect them.

One such high-profile case ended in March 2013, with the sentencing of Thomas Lane for cafeteria murders of three students at Chardon High School in Ohio last year, when Lane was 17. The trial was moved from juvenile to adult court, where Judge David Fuhry gave Lane three consecutive life sentences without any chance of parole.

In Maryland a few weeks earlier, 15-year-old Robert Gladden was convicted of firing a shotgun in the cafeteria at Perry Hall High School and wounding one of his classmates. Tried as an adult, Gladden was sentenced to 35 years in prison.

Gladden's attorney attempted to have the case moved to juvenile court—due to an odd twist in Maryland's law whereby youngsters charged with violent crimes must convince a judge they should not to be held to adult standards—but the defense never had a chance. Although Gladden's and Lane's crimes were committed months before the horrific shootings in Newtown, Conn., each was sentenced after the Sandy Hook rampage and its resulting torrent of emotion and media attention.

The more publicity a youth case receives, the more eager prosecutors seem to be to try it in adult court. Washington, D.C.: five kids await trial as adults in the murder of an 18-year-old in the subway. Raleigh, N.C.: four boys, all age 15, charged as adults in the death of a homeless man. San Jose, Calif.: four teens to be tried as adults in a beating death at a basketball court. The list is long and troubling.

The issue isn't whether violent children should be coddled, nor is it about releasing dangerous individuals, regardless of age, back into society. The fact is we wisely have different judicial standards for children—and those standards should be maintained in all cases, regardless of the severity of a crime or the media attention it receives.

In recent years the U.S. Supreme Court has handed down several decisions that begin to address this, at least at the most extreme levels. In 2005 it barred states from executing anyone for a crime committed as a minor. In 2010 it ruled that no juvenile may be sentenced to life without parole for any crime other than murder. And in 2012 it ruled that children may not be given life sentences unless a judge reviews the specifics of the case and the child's situation.

"Mandatory life without parole for a juvenile precludes consideration of his chronological age and its hallmark features," wrote Justice Elena Kagan in the majority opinion, "among them, immaturity, impetuosity, and failure to appreciate risks and consequences." She added, "It prevents taking into account the family and home environment that surrounds him—and from which he cannot usually extricate himself—no matter how brutal or dysfunctional."

In the 2010 opinion, Justice Anthony Kennedy said there are "fundamental differences between juvenile and adult minds." Indeed, significant research indicates that human psychosocial development isn't fully complete until at least age 22.

The facts are these: roughly 200,000 kids are tried as adults in the U.S. each year. There are currently an estimated 2,000 people serving life sentences, without the chance for parole, for crimes committed before they were 18. The U.S. has the most such prisoners of any developed nation.

While it would be reasonable to incarcerate a convicted juvenile until age 21 and then review carefully his psychological status before considering the ultimate sentence, to prosecute a child and throw away the key is barbaric.

Thomas Lane, the Ohio shooter given three life sentences, is not likely to receive sympathy from many Americans—particularly those who have seen the online video of his grotesque courtroom behavior. But justice is supposed to be blind to such things.

We either acknowledge that children must be treated differently or we don't.

◆◆◆

Obscene Video Violence

The rejection by the U.S. Supreme Court of California's video game law was a welcome victory for free speech, but a frustrating defeat for the protection of young people.

In striking down the 2005 law—that was never actually implemented due to legal challenges—the Court continued its campaign to safeguard the First Amendment. Earlier, it ruled 8-to-1 against a federal law prohibiting depictions of animal cruelty such as those in videos about dog fighting.

But the 7-2 decision voiding the video game law leaves open serious questions. When should First Amendment privileges be suspended for the protection of children? Should a modern interpretation of "obscenity" include violence and not just sex? At what point will ultra-realistic video games be more akin to actual violence and less like the fiction of an earlier era?

These are troubling issues, about which the Supreme Court remains conflicted.

Here's part of the description for the top-selling "Call of Duty: Black Ops II." "Players use pistols, sniper rifles, machine guns, explosives and melee attacks to kill enemy soldiers. Some weapons result in decapitated bodies or dismembered limbs...Other intense acts of violence include a soldier burned alive in a vehicle; a bound man shot in the kneecaps during interrogation; a hostage's throat slit by a villain."

When it comes to protecting children, society takes a wide range of prudent steps—covering everything from voting, to driving, to drinking. Obscenity laws, too, are different for kids, as affirmed by the 1968 Supreme Court ruling that upheld limits on access to sexual materials by minors.

But Justice Antonin Scalia, writing the majority opinion in the video game case, stressed that depiction of violent acts has never been restricted, even for kids. That may be legally correct, but it is morally flawed. As Justice Stephen Breyer said in his dissenting opinion, "What sense does it make to forbid selling to a 13-year-old boy a magazine with an image of a nude woman, while protecting the sale to that 13-year-old of an interactive video game in which he actively, but virtually, binds and gags the woman, then tortures and kills her?"

The Court noted that research on the effects of video games is inconclusive. But many types of causes and effects are difficult to pin down scientifically, which is why the debate raged for decades about the dangers of tobacco, and rambles on today about climate change.

Psychologists face a particularly difficult challenge in evaluating the impact of video gaming because the technology is evolving so rapidly.

Like the definitions of obscenity, which were so subjective at the time of the landmark 1968 ruling as to include the term "girlie magazines," a reasonable evaluation of video violence may hinge more on intuitive reasoning and community standards than on laboratory results. The fact that the U.S. military uses video games for certain forms of combat training should provide a clue about their power.

Here's the crux of the problem, in the very words of Justice Scalia: "Our cases have been clear that the obscenity exception to the First Amendment does not cover whatever a legislature finds shocking, but only depictions of 'sexual conduct.'" That postulate, when children are involved, is shortsighted.

What does it say about society that extreme graphic violence is acceptable for young people, while sex is obscene?

Justice Samuel Alito voted against the California law despite his

concern that the violence in modern video games "is astounding." He said the statute was poorly written, giving too broad a definition of objectionable violent content. However, Alito seemed to suggest that California legislators could draft a new law spelling out more clearly the narrow range of video violence that should be off limits to kids. They should.

Alito wisely added, "developing technology may have important societal implications that will become apparent only with time."

Safeguarding free speech and protecting our children need not be in conflict. However, waiting for scientific evidence of the "societal implications" about which Justice Alito warns, is a game that responsible adults cannot afford to play.

CRISSCROSSING THE COUNTRY

Smile Index

I took a three-week trip, mostly by car, covering thousands of miles and sampling hundreds of opinions. I went to big cities—LA, Chicago, Washington, New York and Boston—and small towns—from Lancaster, Calif., to Lenox, Mass. And what I found in my unscientific sample was that despite miserable economic conditions and a severe political divide, Americans remain remarkably resilient.

Maybe I was influenced by late summer's burst of perfect weather and resulting Kodachrome views—from the 95th floor of the John Hancock building in Chicago looking out over a glistening Lake Michigan, to the lawn at Tanglewood in Lenox, as the Boston Symphony concluded its season with Beethoven's rousing "Ode to Joy." Perhaps it was the pleasingly peaceful behavior of a large gathering near the Washington Monument, which, considering the harsh opinions unleashed, could have turned violent. Maybe it was President Obama going on TV to declare that the most nightmarish aspects of America's fighting in its two long-running wars seem to be behind us.

Or maybe it was just that the ice cream at Handel's landmark stand in Youngstown, Ohio, was so enjoyable on an evening when the breeze was warm and the mint chip sweet.

With gas prices lower than the summer before (although in New England, taxes make a gallon cost so much more in Connecticut and New York than in Massachusetts), many Americans were on the road. In some spots the traffic was jammed, but often for good cause, since federal stimulus money continued to fund some 12,000 highway projects, creating construction jobs along the way.

Still, roughly 12 million Americans are out of work, and many are hurting because of it. I saw a shopping plaza not far from Tanglewood that was 75% vacant. Even on bucolic Main Street in New Canaan, Conn., family-owned shops were closing at an alarming rate.

Up and down the Salinas Valley in Central California, where the air is thick with dust, thousands of workers dotted the fields, with scarves protecting their faces and hats blocking the sun, hunched over for hours to pick our lettuce and broccoli. They ride to and from the fields in old buses that look just like the vehicles used to transport prisoners to nearby Soledad prison. Some politicians want to send many of the field workers back to Mexico, based on the misguided notion that there are Americans eager to take these backbreaking jobs.

At O'Toole's in Chicago, diehard fans continued to cheer for their hapless Cubs, who on this day managed to lose, 16-5, to the Braves. Despite the economic slump, there were big crowds at the mall in Providence, R.I., with the wait for a table at the Cheesecake Factory running an hour or longer, as many people enjoyed an end-of-summer treat.

At all these stops I used my own Smile Index to measure the mood of people I met. Most seemed resigned. There's almost a palpable sense that we're all in this together, and it shows up in the way folks smile and say hello.

Indeed, it was all on display one Saturday morning at the Cafe on the Common in Mansfield, Mass., where the breakfast is terrific and the cheerful service is even better. It was the first week of school football, and the place was packed. But those seated at the window could look straight across the town green at families standing in the sun, waiting for a free meal at the food pantry run by a local church.

A few miles up the road in Norton, a guy was standing at an intersection with a folding table and a large poster that read: "Impeach Obama." I didn't stop to talk, but I could see he wasn't happy.

That's too bad, because America's got a lot going for it, and President Obama isn't part of the problem, he's helping to provide the solutions. What I see is a nation that feels slightly safer, resigned to tough it out, and hoping we're turning the corner.

That same week, as the president returned from his own vacation, he got a look at the new rug in the Oval Office on which appear five memorable quotes from great Americans. One is from Teddy Roosevelt: "The welfare of each of us is dependent fundamentally upon the welfare of all of us."

And whether your vantage point is an exit on the Interstate, or standing on the White House rug, the vision is of renewed hope in America.

◆◆◆

Signs of Confusion

In an age when Twitterphiles are able to communicate deep thoughts with just 140 characters, it's puzzling that the authors of highway signs so often struggle to make sense.

Zigzagging my way from Virginia to Massachusetts I encountered numerous signs that were impossible to decipher. For instance, on I-95 near Quantico Marine Base in Virginia there's a big sign that says: End Highway Safety Corridor. What could that possibly mean?

Should drivers assume it's now OK to drive recklessly? Do police stop enforcing safety regulations beyond that point?

On I-495 near Silver Spring, Md., a sign reads: DUI Enforcement Area. Really? I've been driving under the assumption that every foot of roadway in America is a DUI Enforcement Area.

With so many motorists distracted nowadays by personal electronic gadgets—plus, of course, arguing with their spouses, fielding the kids' questions, eating, applying makeup, etc.—the last thing we need is signage that persons of reasonable intelligence can't understand. Worse, we don't need information that we're powerless to do anything about.

On the Massachusetts Turnpike near Westover AFB in Chicopee, there are signs saying: Caution Low-Flying Aircraft. I don't recall any tips in the drivers' manual about avoiding airplanes. It would make just as much sense to post a warning about periodic meteor showers. Besides, if a plane is so low that it threatens a five-foot high Pontiac then it's probably a little late for a written warning.

What does a road sign cost anyway? About $75? Then what's the point of installing a $75 sign to warn of a bump that would probably cost about $50 to repair?

On the highway heading to Freehold, N.J., I saw a permanent sign that said: Trees Sprayed with Noxious Spray. Aside from the fact that the sign maker apparently had a tough time finding a synonym for "spray" ("treated" might have worked), what are motorists to do? Turn back? Hold their breath? For how long?

Many highway signs are of little or no value to the driving public, but are posted for convoluted legal purposes so that government agencies can avoid culpability. I suppose when sued over the noxious sprays in New Jersey, government can say, "Well, we warned you." The same is true with the Highway Safety Corridor. Apparently it's an area in which traffic fines are doubled—and there's a legal reason to notify motorists that they've reached the end of that section.

Across Maryland, troubling signs of the times are posted on giant electronic boards. They give an 800 phone number and advise: Report Suspicious Activity. What's that about? Should I report the guy who just cut in front of me at 90 mph? Or by "suspicious" do they mean, say, Arab-looking motorists who might have a package in the trunk that could be a bomb?

These digital, or "smart" highway signs are sometimes pretty dumb. On the New Jersey Turnpike—as in several states—electronic speed signs are left blank when there are no dangerous conditions. On such occasions the signs say SPEED LIMIT with no numbers posted, leaving motorists confused about what the proper speed really is. In some states the electric signs have resulted in varying speeds being posted in different lanes on the same highway.

Apparently the sign situation is so frustrating that a few motorists feel the need to inject comic relief. In Greenville, Del., the computer for an electric highway sign was hacked and the message changed to: Live Nudes Ahead.

In Maryland, there's a highway overpass with the sign: Brooklyn Bridge Road. Someone with spray paint and a sense of humor added: 4 Sale.

And what's coming? A headline in the Albany, N.Y., *Times Union* warned: "Confusing road signs about to hit the highway."

◆◆◆

Up Front in America

Most Saturday mornings, just for fun and without spending a dime on gas, I take a trip to roughly 100 American cities and towns.

I do this through a terrific website operated by the Newseum, a facility in Washington, D.C., dedicated to preserving and promoting the nation's news media, particularly its daily newspapers. At www.newseum.org there is a section called Today's Front Pages which, without comment or embellishment, lets visitors read newspaper "fronts" from around the nation.

During one of my tours I saw on the front page of *The Durango Herald* in Colorado that residents were complaining about the city's 50-foot pile of snow that was collected during winter and turned brown and smelly and wouldn't seem to melt, global warming and the coming of summer notwithstanding.

The Courier News in New Jersey reported the four millionth fan to attend a Somerset Patriots minor-league baseball game received a year's supply of Ben & Jerry's ice cream. *The Stamford Advocate* in Connecticut ran a photo of a 2000 Jeep Cherokee, bought by a local man for $26,000 because it was once owned by Barack Obama.

In Georgia, *The Gainesville Times* led with news that Scott Haley, 28, was sentenced to two years in prison for posting YouTube videos in which he claimed, falsely, to have killed 16 people in what the paper noted, "could be the first case of its kind in Georgia." There was legal news in North Dakota as well where *The Bismarck Tribune* told about a guy who was protesting because state officials wouldn't allow his personalized license plate to read ISNOGOD.

In an eye-catching photo on page one of the *Herald News* in Fall River, Mass., "chain saw artist" Jesse Green was shown making a wooden sculpture of chef Emeril Lagasse, of all people.

According to *The Press Journal* in Indian River, Fla., an 86-year-old page of math homework was found at the former Fellsmere School building. "So all these years later," the story said, "Hallie Alcutt could prove that she really did lose her homework." Unfortunately, Ms. Alcutt died eight years ago at age 91.

In Albany, N.Y., *The Times Union* reported that a middle school sparked controversy by banning hugging on campus. Meanwhile in

Georgia, a front-page story in the *Macon Telegraph* said several parents were turned away at high school graduation ceremonies for wearing short pants.

It was front-page news in Riverside, California's *Press-Enterprise* that Jordan Romero, 13, became the youngest person to climb Mount Everest. Other mountains made news, as *The Honolulu Star Bulletin* ran a photo of the Kilauea Volcano erupting for the 10,000th straight day.

As different as the nation's front pages tend to be, it's clear that all editors love photos of animals. On this single Saturday, moose were fronted on *The Anchorage Daily News* and bison on *The New York Times*. There was a goat on *The Harrison Daily Times* in Arkansas, a horse on *The Washington Post*, and a giant octopus on *The Telegraph Herald* in Dubuque, Iowa. *The Erie Times-News* in Pennsylvania featured a colony of bees, *The State* in Columbia, S.C. focused on kangaroos, and *The Wisconsin State Journal* pictured a monkey.

Under the headline "Pooch in the Pokey," *The Union* in Grass Valley, Calif., disclosed that a pit bull named Romeo may have been framed for attacks on neighborhood pets. In Iowa, the lead item in the *Sioux City Journal* was that a cat named Amazing Grace survived surgery to remove a three-inch nail from her head.

In other news of good fortune, *The Topeka Capital-Journal* in Kansas reported that Donna Nish found 21 four-leaf clovers and three five-leaf clovers growing in her front yard.

The Times Record in Fort Smith, Ark., revealed that a program requiring drunk drivers to tour prisons is running into trouble because many of them are showing up for the tours drunk.

Then there was the story on the front page of the *Courier-Times* in New Castle, Ind., announcing plans for the annual Memorial Day celebration. The highlight was to be a traveling museum about funerals. Reporter Donna Cronk noted that alongside the caskets "there will be complimentary hot dogs, chips, beverages, and tropical shaved ice."

It's apparent that despite the shrinking globe, this remains a remarkably diverse nation. And despite technological changes in the news business, the nation's front pages still capture it best.

◆◆◆

Vendor of Smiles

PHOENIX—This is not about politics or the economy, at least not directly. This is about Lemonade. "Lemonade, lemonade, like grandma made!"

For nearly three decades, Derrick Moore has been selling drinks at sports venues across the West, but quenching thirst is only part of his mission. Moore is arguably the nation's top ballpark vendor of smiles.

Fans attending games in Arizona, Southern California and Nevada—over 250 events each year—often can't remember the final score, but they never forget Moore's deep, rousing call: "Lemonade, Lemonade, like grandma made!"

As by far the most popular vendor in baseball's springtime Cactus League, Moore has his pick of venues, so lately he's been following the World Champion Giants. Wherever they play, that's where Moore peddles his good cheer. "Yummy, yummy. You know you want it!"

During the regular season, Moore is so popular at Diamondbacks (baseball), Suns (basketball) and Cardinals (football) games that fans seek his autograph, pose with him in photos, and even plead with the smiling "Lemonade Guy" to record messages on their cellphones—"like grandma made!" In the fall he travels to San Diego for Chargers football and to Nevada for college games and monster truck races.

For 17 years, Moore was a beer vendor ("Get a cold brew, you know what to do!"). He made a good living to support his wife and four kids at their home north of Phoenix, but he grew frustrated by the often-rowdy behavior of the beer-drinking crowd. It also didn't square with his faith. Moore is a religious man who ministers to prison inmates and troubled youngsters in his spare time.

In 2002 Moore gave up beer and switched to lemonade. He says his grandma Beulah made some of the best lemonade in Phoenix and most folks who stopped by for a cool drink left with a smile. So Moore fashioned his sales approach around memories of his late grandma.

On a good day he sells 300 lemonades, roughly twice the number the average soft drink vendor can score. He works for three different lemonade companies, each with its own t-shirt, so he has to be sure to wear the correct uniform when he switches venues.

At some stadiums the price is $5, at others it's $5.75, and rookie vendors prefer the higher price because customers usually let them keep the 25-cents change. But Moore takes a hit at $5.75, since his frequent tip for a $5 drink is a full dollar.

At a spring training game in Peoria, Moore strolled through the stands entertaining fans while a rogue beer vendor followed behind calling, "Miller Lite, like grandpa used to drink." A few aisles away, a competing lemonade vendor shouted, "Lemonade, just like Derrick's grandma made!" Moore didn't object; he was flattered.

A Phoenix radio station and a local car dealer hired him to do commercials. He travels two hours to sell at concerts and festivals in Tucson ("Limonada, limonada, like nana used to make!").

During spring training he will sometimes do both a day game and a night game, leaving his voice hoarse and his back sore—yet his wide grin is unaffected. When Moore preaches in jails the theme is about curbing anger and bitterness; in ballparks there's no need for a sermon, but the message is the same.

"It doesn't matter what you do for a living," he says, "as long as you love it. I go to work happy, and I leave work feeling even happier. I enjoy making people smile." With a deep chuckle, he adds the trademark, "Yeah, baby!"

Life handed Derrick Moore a lemon, and grandma Beulah would be pleased to know he's making lemonade, mixed with good cheer.

◆◆◆

BETWEEN THE COVERS

Closing the Book

I used to have an aversion to big-box stores, especially those that destroy well-run, friendly neighborhood businesses, which is a fundamental part of the big-box strategy.

Over time my stance softened. My family and I do more of our shopping in places like Target, Best Buy, Costco and Home Depot, because of the large selection and reasonable prices. Yes, the personal touch is missing—but that's a tradeoff, because sometimes you want to spend an hour examining dozens of socket wrenches without a salesperson hovering.

When the Borders company opened its cavernous bookstore in our community, circa 1999, I was even more conflicted. I hated what would predictably happen to our local bookshops and, sure enough, most of them died slow and financially painful deaths. On the other hand, it was a wonderful new experience to plop down in a bookstore and actually peruse a chapter without feeling guilty.

Our Borders was as box-like as a big-box could be. It wasn't even in a mall; it was at the edge of town in a retail development that contained a half-dozen mega-stores and a few fast-food shops. It was part of the sprawl that is wrecking Downtown, America.

But there were so many books! Plus, newspapers and magazines, DVDs and CDs—and a coffee shop where local authors gave lectures and music groups performed. It seemed to be the type of place that would help preserve books and periodicals, not contribute to their demise.

From its inception, Borders was a poorly managed business. It was plagued by supply problems, causing key titles to be missing for many days. It was slow to adapt to new technology—both online and with e-books. It had an awful "rewards" program that provided little value to loyal customers.

Yet, the more than 600 Borders stores were havens. I recall rushing into the Providence, R.I., store when I needed a book about birds, with lots of color pictures, for the seven-year-old son of a friend I was visiting. They had a dozen from which to choose, and free giftwrapping.

I remember spending part of an afternoon at the branch in Scottsdale, Ariz., when the temperature outside was over 100. I perused dozens of out-of-town newspapers, enjoyed the air conditioning, and purchased a book for my wife about identifying wild mushrooms.

In San Francisco, I used to visit the Borders store across the street from AT&T Park while waiting for a Giants game. I'd go to the big branch just off Union Square and sit at a wooden table on the second floor reading parts of several books that seemed interesting, but weren't quite worth owning.

Then one day it all disappeared. And no matter what the digital future holds in delivering books via electronic devices, losing Borders can't be viewed as a good thing. Beyond the 10,700 staffers who joined the growing ranks of unemployed; beyond the wreckage of local bookshops that couldn't hang on during Borders' meteoric rise, and beyond the blight of shuttered Borders' venues across the map, the fabric of society is being ripped a bit more.

As I said, Borders was not a well-run company, so perhaps a highly paid publicist rather than a lover of literature crafted the following bit of prose. Regardless, here's what it said on the Borders website just before it was shuttered:

"We are passionate about the importance of literacy and knowledge to our culture; dedicated to the extraordinary power of books—those who write them, read them, collect them, look after them, treasure them."

Earlier, as it came clear that Borders was struggling, I wrote in *The Wall Street Journal* that the crumbling of some big-box operations might actually create an opportunity for small, locally operated bookstores. I theorized that with the bulk of business shifting to online merchants and electronic reading devices, there would still be a niche for stores where you could hold a book in your hands while sipping coffee, listening to music, and savoring the experience in a way that Amazon and Kindle simply can't provide.

I hope I was right. As badly as I felt when Borders first came to town, the feeling was even worse when it left.

Save Our Books!

DENVER—A protest by students at the University of Denver was eye-opening because of how it was conducted, what it achieved and, most of all, what it concerned.

Students here demanded more books.

Activism at DU has a rich history, including the anti-war protest in 1970 known as Woodstock West, and the earlier Coffee Break Riot of 1965. In the '65 incident, passion was roused after the administration ended the morning coffee break, a 50-minute period during which no classes were conducted. Students blocked traffic, lit fires and battled with police, but failed to win back their caffeine privileges. It was an era when everything was a Big Deal, and the mood on many campuses was volatile.

Returning to my alma mater, I was fascinated by the latest protest. It seems DU's campus library was badly in need of repairs and modernization. When plans for a $32-million renovation were announced, they revealed that most of the books, about 800,000 volumes, would disappear. These books would be stored at an off-campus location, and be accessible via special order only.

DU, like many universities, was seeking to adapt to changing needs and conditions. The new facility would house more computers, a million e-books and other digital resources. Space that had been used to shelve books would be used for new study areas—reflecting another trend on campuses in which students seek to escape the hubbub of dormitories and increasingly prefer the gentle buzz of a busy, but orderly study environment. Rather than just calling it a "library," DU refers to its new structure as an "academic commons."

To the administration's surprise, students immediately challenged the plan and, relying upon mainly the tools of social networking, launched a protest. Their leader, Brandon Reich-Sweet, said the plan "jeopardized the academic vitality of this institution." More fundamentally, he asked: "What is a library?"

It was here in Denver a few years earlier that Suzanne Thorin, dean of libraries at Syracuse University, told a gathering of educators, "The library, as a place, is dead. Kaput. Finito. And we need to move on to a new concept of what the academic library is."

DU students clearly disagreed. "What surprised us about the protest," I learned from Anne McCall, the dean of Arts & Humanities, "is that it wasn't the older graduate students who were most concerned, it was the younger students, the freshman and sophomores. They wanted more books in the library."

Following a series of Save the Library demonstrations, one student wrote about it in the campus newspaper, *The Clarion*, under the headline, "Has DU forgotten about books?"

"There is something about being surrounded by books," said Kathy Owens. "Friends, adventures and information at the tip of your fingers, far more tangible than an article a few clicks away on your computer."

This was refreshing stuff to hear from a college student, especially for those of us who are still in shock over the equivalent changes in our off-campus world where Borders Books along with hundreds of smaller independent book retailers have disappeared and left us with primarily electronic and online alternatives. And it's not as if the students are out of step with digital changes. Another *Clarion* carried an opinion column that criticized professors who ban laptops in class. Also, the new library has 1,864 power outlets for students using personal electronics.

Reich-Sweet, the student activist, noted that losing the library books was "just a small symbol of a broader cultural trend. The scribbles and sounds we interpret as 'library' would have begun to lose all meaning."

In the end, DU's administration yielded, at least part way, and returned over 500,000 books to the spiffy new library shelves.

As an observer, it's hard to decide what means more: the restoration of books to the very place they belong? Or the fact that students took such an honorable approach, using the tech tools of a modern age, to protect and preserve the past?

It's quite a victory. And Denver alums who recall the protests of the mid-'60s will be pleased to know that the new library not only has books—it also serves coffee.

◆◆◆

Break the College Textbook Racket

My son's college textbook and work book for Spanish class cost $200, which in any language is un mal negocio (a bad deal).

Despite student petitions, digital options and congressional intervention, the tab for textbooks keeps growing in what is now an $8 billion industry. Prices are so high that some college students, as reported in *USA Today*, are trying to get by without purchasing the required books.

Why is something so fundamental as the price of a school book so difficult to control?

The College Board places the average annual cost of books at $1,168 per student. Efforts to reduce this staggering sum have led to marketing of used, rental and various forms of electronic books. But there are many hurdles, and the textbook situation is likely to get worse before it gets better.

Although college enrollment has increased in the past 10 years, textbook sales have been dropping. Not surprisingly, publishers and authors will do whatever they can to maintain profit levels. So, for example, as sales of used books have increased, prices for new books have climbed.

E-books cost less to produce than printed texts, yet they don't change the bottom line dramatically. For one thing, they are sold separately to each user, eliminating used books and shared copies. And they require hardware, which students or schools must purchase and maintain.

Some smaller publishers have begun offering "open-source" books, distributed online for free. These suppliers make their money by selling study aids and other supplements, but it is not clear whether such a model can succeed on a larger scale.

There are also indications that many students still prefer printed books. This is likely to change over time, but it means e-books must be introduced gradually.

College bookstores profit from sales, as do some professors who make students buy books they have written. Also, teachers seem too willing to require new, "revised" editions of textbooks, even though the changes could be minimal. In doing so, they wipe out the market for used copies.

The Higher Education Opportunity Act, which took effect at the start of the 2010 school year, included several provisions aimed at easing the cost of textbooks. For instance, colleges are required to identify all books for a course at the time of registration so students can evaluate the costs, and publishers must offer texts separately, rather than bundling them with CDs or workbooks.

A congressional advisory committee identified several factors that inflate prices. The most damaging is that the primary choosers of books are not the primary users; that is, teachers usually select the books, but students pay for them. Second, students often are resigned to hikes in prices because they are generally hostage to professors' selections. Interestingly, many European schools demand lower prices from publishers. The committee discovered that one popular economics textbook cost $126 in the U.S. but $76 in Great Britain.

A good first step in controlling college book costs would be for schools to comply with the law. Another would be for administrators to insist that teachers avoid ordering new editions that offer only cosmetic changes.

Ultimately, wider use of electronic formats will loosen the grip of a few large publishing companies, leading to greater competition and presumably lower prices. Meanwhile, colleges and universities should wake up to the fact that the best way to avoid having $200 books is to stop requiring students to buy them.

A new chapter in textbook pricing can't be written quickly enough.

LEARNING ABOUT EDUCATION

For Kids, All Work Won't Work

If the worst thing that all work and no play does is make Jack a dull boy, then Jack is luckier than most. For many American youngsters too much schoolwork is making them overweight, out of shape, and dangerously sleep-deprived.

With over 55 million students enrolled in grades K to 12, it's fair to say that some American schools are succeeding in finding a balance between scholastics and health. But the trend lines are troubling.

What if an adult business executive described this routine: I work a full shift during the day, and then I bring home at least 5 hours of work in the evening; I get about 20 percent less sleep than experts recommend; my lunch is grabbed during a 30-minute dash between assignments; I've eliminated my daily hour of physical conditioning.

This exec would be counseled that his life and career are at great risk. As the headline on a *Wall Street Journal* advice column put it: "If You Need to Work Better, Maybe Try Working Less."

Why do we treat students differently? Is it because many public schools are overly focused on one-size-fits-all scholastic standards? Is it because parents are obsessed with college competition? Is it because budget cuts have stripped away physical education programs and other after-school activities? If you answered "all of the above," we're on the same page.

I put pencil to paper to compute the scheduling conundrum that faced my 17-year-old son during his junior year. According to Brown University's research, he should get between 9 and 9.25 hours of sleep each night. To arrive at school on time, he must wake up no later than 6:15 a.m., so he should be asleep by 9 p.m.

At his well-funded, highly ranked public high school in central California he is offered no physical education classes. He is given 35 minutes for lunch, but school clubs use this precious break period for meetings, thus squeezing the actual meal time to a mad race. Although the school sets homework rules for most classes, it refuses to provide any guidelines for advanced placement and honors courses. On any given night, that means he might have an hour of work per subject—over five hours total.

Back to my chart. If he leaves school immediately after his last class, he can be home by 3:45 p.m. (although many classmates are not so lucky). He now has five hours and 15 minutes of waking time left, and over five hours of homework.

Can he spend, say, 30 minutes playing outside? Can we allow him 45 minutes for dinner with the family? Should he do any chores around the house? Is a single TV program or video game completely out of the question? Something—indeed, everything—has to give.

The crux of this scheduling problem would seem to be the sleep requirement. If my son could get by on 20 percent less sleep he could probably make it all work. But according to Judith Owens of Brown, just 2.5 percent of the population needs less sleep than average. "The problem," she told The New York Times, "is that 95 percent of us think we're in that 2.5 percent." She advises parents to assume their kids need the full amount of sleep until it is proven otherwise.

When it comes to homework, Duke University's widely accepted research shows that students do, in fact, achieve more when home-work is part of their scholastic routine—but only to a point. That point, according to researchers, comes at about two hours per night in 12th grade.

In communities where competition for good grades and a ticket to a big-name college is keen, parents are often hooted out of the room for suggesting that homework be kept to a reasonable limit, that time be found in the school day for all students to get some exercise, and that good nutrition must be more than just a catch phrase.

Mental and physical fitness need not be mutually exclusive in our schools. While it is generally acknowledged that American students need to achieve more to compete nationally and globally, all work and little play is not the lesson.

"Youth is wasted on the young," observed George Bernard Shaw. Increasingly, we are requiring youth to be wasted by the young as well.

◆◆◆

A Wiki Education

Educators concerned over the digital revolution's impact on schools should review two notable quotes that have kicked around for decades.

The first came from the renowned journalist A.J. Liebling, who wrote in *The New Yorker*, "Freedom of the press is guaranteed only to those who own one." Liebling made the observation in 1960, before the Internet and digital technology began the process of turning printing presses into museum pieces.

The second is attributed to Senator Daniel Patrick Moynihan of New York, who famously noted, "Everyone is entitled to their own opinion, but not to their own facts." Moynihan said it before the term "wiki" entered the lexicon, forever blurring matters of fact.

The ability to self-publish and to be simultaneously reckless with facts should raise a warning flag for all modern communicators, but nowhere is the need for caution greater than in education.

A shift from printed textbooks to electronic formats is well under way and is, for the most part, a good thing. But a wrinkle is the ease with which digital teaching materials can be altered, even distorted, by users.

Publisher McGraw-Hill operates a division called Create, through which teachers can design their own textbooks. The primary resource for these texts is McGraw-Hill's library of over 4,000 books and 5,500 articles, from which content is culled electronically to create a new book. The finished product is available in both printed form and as an e-book.

In creating their own volumes, teachers are able to delete portions of existing texts and intersperse their own writings and notes. The benefit of giving individual teachers such power is likely to depend not only on their expertise and skill, but also on such factors as their political and religious beliefs.

Teacher discretion about course material has always varied among schools and districts, even when old-fashioned printed texts were the only option. Yet, the statewide or district-wide approval process for books tends to provide a framework in which teachers must operate. It also gives students the clarity and comfort that comes from a larger, usually more accomplished, authority.

That's not to say that textbooks aren't already facing criticism in many regions. In Texas, for example, books have been modified by state order to reflect revised views about such things as taxes, separation of church and state, and what Texas officials have deemed are the "unintended consequences" of affirmative action. This is troublesome enough without giving rogue teachers the power to tailor texts to suit a particular agenda.

Even the Texas Board of Education stopped short of adopting a proposal that would have required all textbooks to refer to President Obama only by his full name, Barack Hussein Obama. But if an individual teacher wishes to have it read that way in a self-published e-book, it can be done with a few keystrokes.

The Wikimedia Foundation, operator of the enormously popular Wikipedia Internet encyclopedia, has a companion site known as Wikibooks, containing roughly 2,700 online textbooks that, the site proudly proclaims, "anyone can edit." In an announcement aimed at educators, Wikibooks describes itself as "uniquely suited for use in classroom collaborative projects."

Is it possible that while many teachers flatly prohibit students from using Wikipedia for research because of its very wiki nature, some would embrace Wikibooks as "uniquely suited" for inclusion in class?

The shift into the digital world is not only inevitable; it is essential to the larger task of modernizing and elevating America's standing in education. However, with each new tool comes the requirement for caution.

It is true that a press is no longer needed to publish. But it remains unequivocal that no one is entitled to his own facts, especially in the classroom.

◆◆◆

Where Did Journalism Classes Go?

While the newspaper industry worries about shrinking print editions and uncertain economics in the digital world, an equally vexing issue lurks. Where will the next generation's journalists come from, and how well will they be trained?

In speaking to a workshop for award-winning high school reporters from across California, I was dismayed to learn how many of their schools have dropped journalism courses and cut back or eliminated student newspapers. In the last decade over 200 high schools in California have scrubbed journalism.

Nationally, the situation is similarly worrisome. According to Anita Luera, a director at the Walter Cronkite School of Journalism in Arizona, "Many high school journalism programs have suffered in recent years, the victim of budget cuts and other priorities, especially at schools with large minority populations."

But beyond budgets, the increasingly rigid focus on core subjects and standardized tests has made some valuable electives, such as journalism, less important to high school administrators. That's not only a shame, it's misguided.

A study by the Newspaper Association of America showed that students who worked on high school papers and yearbooks scored better on college admission tests and tended to have higher grades in their first year of college.

Notably, while the journalism trend line is plunging at high schools, it is actually rising at the college level. At Northwestern's Medill School of Journalism, for example, the number of graduates is up by about 25 percent over the last decade; at the University of Missouri, the journalism school graduating classes are up 40 percent during the same period.

At these colleges, journalism is a core area of study, with its own revenue base. But at many high schools these days, news writing is viewed as more like, say, the cheerleading squad—the difference being few high school administrators would ever dare cut the cheerleading budget.

Some high schools that have managed to maintain student papers have cut frequency to monthly or quarterly. As a result, the publications become more feature and opinion oriented, while lacking hard news. This tends to feed the very problems that young writers face in the expanding online world, where everyone has an opinion and the glorious freedom to express it, but too often without proper discipline in reporting, editing and fact-checking. It's difficult to develop a serious regard for these components of responsible journalism if there are no classes to teach them, and if the school paper, produced by an under-funded after-school club, doesn't encourage them.

As I spoke with individual students at the workshop, the knowledge gap between those whose schools offered journalism and those for whom it was no longer available was stunning. It's difficult to imagine the latter group succeeding in college journalism courses.

Even at colleges where journalism programs appear to be thriving, there are subtle shifts in curriculum that put less emphasis on the fundamentals of good reporting. Many schools, for example, are combining basic journalism with video and computer classes, where the focus tends to be more on the medium than the message. Sadly, this mirrors what is happening in the consumer marketplace.

As journalism's economic and delivery models change at the professional level, it is more important than ever for colleges and high schools to ground students in the principles of good writing and reporting. Communities must find the means to restore high school journalism programs, lest the pipelines that flow to colleges and the professional world run dry.

Many observers of the current media scene fret for good reason about the careless, even reckless, state of what often passes for news in burgeoning outlets on the Internet and cable-TV dial. Journalists in the next generation can't be counted upon to improve things unless they at least know better.

◆◆◆

Protecting School Kids

Jonathan Hornik, the Democratic mayor of Marlboro Township in New Jersey, is a pragmatist. He favors a ban on the sale of assault weapons. He also wants laws to prohibit ordinary citizens from possessing high-capacity magazines. He supports recommendations from

Vice President Joe Biden's task force for additional ways to curb the epidemic of gun violence in the U.S.

But realizing that these essential steps will take time, Hornik took action to protect the 8,000 children in his community by stationing a uniformed police officer in each school until further notice.

The gun issue is one of the most divisive in America. The mere mention of new gun laws incites harsh commentary on both sides, and on Capitol Hill the topic is more radioactive than taxes, the deficit or even war.

However, the issue of school safety goes beyond guns. When it comes to kids, what matters is protecting them while their elders struggle to find better societal solutions for maintaining their safety.

Following the Newtown tragedy, the notion of placing cops in schools was immediately politicized because it was among things advocated by the NRA's notorious leader, Wayne LaPierre. Gun opponents immediately challenge anything the NRA suggests—much as any proposal to limit gun ownership is contested by Second Amendment fundamentalists. LaPierre is a lousy spokesman, even for his own cause, and his choice of words—"good guys with guns"—only serves to confuse matters when it comes to stationing police at schools.

Officials like Mayor Hornik are not proposing arming civilians, as the notorious sheriff Joe Arpaio seeks to do in Arizona. They're talking about stationing uniformed town police officers at schools, just as they are sent to patrol ballparks, malls, airports, etc. Hornik's rationale is spot on when he says that the cops "will give our students comfort, our town and community comfort, and will have anybody think twice about coming into Marlboro schools."

Yet those who disagree with this simple logic deliberately distort the issue in their choice of words. For instance, they persist in using the term "armed guards," even though town police would never be referred to that way in routine performance of their duties. New Jersey Governor Chris Christie says having a cop on duty would make schools "armed camps." How ridiculous. More than 20 percent of the nation's public schools already have a city or town cop present, and the facilities are no more armed camps than Yankee Stadium is when New York cops patrol during games.

Some say uniformed police would send the wrong message to kids. Why? Youngsters should be taught that cops are their friends—people they must rush to if they ever encounter trouble in public.

Opponents make much of the fact that in 1999 a deputy stationed at Columbine High in Colorado failed to thwart gunmen who killed 12 students. But no form of police protection is perfect. Gunmen got to John Kennedy and Ronald Reagan, but that's certainly no reason to stop providing protection for presidents.

It is often mentioned that hiring cops is expensive, especially for small communities. That's a matter of local priorities, although I would advocate a federal program to assist municipalities in paying for officers in schools.

"My first choice would be to never have a gun in our schools," explained Mayor Hornik, "but while the President and the NRA and the Congress debate policy and law, the fact is there are guns out there. How many times do we have to see these kinds of mass shootings before we decide to protect our kids?"

Hornik's position is not a concession to the NRA, nor should it detract from the critical issue of gun control.

If a public building were to be used to store several hundred gold bars, stationing a cop at the door wouldn't spark so much as a syllable of debate. Why do we think less of a school containing several hundred precious children?

◆◆◆

Fake 'Honors' Con Kids

Thousands of high school students received "invitations" to attend each of Barack Obama's inaugurations in Washington. But in many cases the trips were organized by unscrupulous marketers who engage in year-round travel scams aimed at students and their families.

"You have been selected to represent your state at the Presidential Youth Leadership Conference...Your selection is in recognition of your academic achievement...Witness Barack Obama take the Presidential Oath of Office...listen while he gives his Presidential Address."

So reads a letter to students across the nation, many of whom would reasonably assume they have earned something beyond the chance to pay a marketing firm exorbitant fees. In fact, the "selection" carries about as much weight as a Publishers Clearing House letter advising, "You may already be a winner!"

What is confounding about these youth programs is that they have so successfully convinced educators, students, parents, and even elected officials of their worth, despite clear evidence that they are rip-offs. Adding to the deception, many of the firms operate as nonprofit organizations—creating the appearance of benevolence—while, in fact, siphoning huge profits to for-profit companies run by the same people.

Envision EMI, a for-profit firm based in Virginia, operated by direct-marketing guru Richard Rossi, runs several programs including Congressional Youth Leadership Council and National Youth Leadership Forum. The "Genius Network" website credits Rossi with writing one direct mail package to students that "produced over 100 million dollars in revenue."

Another for-profit company, Lead America, runs almost identical programs - including the "Presidential" conference - with fees as high as $6,000. Both firms trade on the same emotions, selling overpriced

trips with fancy direct-mail "invitations," suggesting that entry consti-
tutes an "honor," when in fact none exists.

To test Lead America's claim that its "nominations" are based
upon merit, I emailed the firm using a fictitious name, stating that although my son was "only a C student," I would gladly pay if he could
attend an event. A few days later a lavish color brochure arrived along
with a "Certificate of Acceptance" citing my son's "academic excel-
lence, extracurricular involvement and leadership potential." In addition to the tuition, I was offered the chance to buy a Leadership Home
Study Kit for $259 ("a 35% savings"), and a $100 insurance policy to
cover refunding my money if the event was canceled.

A few weeks later, my fictitious son received a glossy invitation to
the Obama inauguration, stating that he was "selected" based upon
"academic achievement." The price: $2,395. The fine print: travel to
Washington, D.C. is not included, nor is admission to any Inaugural
events.

In fact, tickets to presidential inaugurations are available only
through Congress. At the request of Sen. Dianne Feinstein's Inaugural
Committee, eBay agreed to pull all offers of inauguration tickets.

Years ago, Senators Howard Metzenbaum (D-Ohio) and Robert
Dole (R-Kan.) introduced legislation to force the Congressional Youth
Leadership Council and similar programs to explain how participants
were chosen and how their money is spent. Despite impassioned arguments by Dole, the bill was never enacted; nor was a similar House
measure.

Dole did succeed in persuading many of his colleagues in Congress
to insist that their names be removed from literature naming them as
"Honorary Advisors" to the programs. Incredibly, 15 years later, both
Envision and Lead America still distribute the literature—now containing names of nearly 400 elected officials, including House Democratic Leader Nancy Pelosi and Senate Majority Leader Harry Reid.

I brought this to the attention of my Congressman, Rep. Sam Farr
(D-CA), and his aides have since succeeded in having Farr's name removed from Lead America's literature.

As competition for college admission has increased, bogus programs that claim to give students an edge have mushroomed. Once
their name gets on a list, some high school students receive dozens of

impressive "invitations" from "Honor Societies" and "Youth Leadership" organizations, selling little more than false hopes.

Perhaps the saddest aspect of the marketing scheme run by Lead America comes in a document on its website, encouraging youngsters to appeal to local businesses in their hometowns for money to help them achieve their "honor." If that fails, the document encourages students to run errands, hold bake sales, or "sell flowers" to pay fees.

Some students do enjoy these overpriced trips, while others find them mismanaged failures. Either way, the emotions hinge on the false assumption that youngsters achieved elite status and were selected through legitimate process for a true scholastic honor.

Congress should take another look at these scams and, at minimum, remove from marketing materials the names of elected officials who don't endorse the programs. Students, meanwhile, should learn a simple lesson that comes at no charge: when "honors" seem too good to be true, they usually are.

If I Ran a High School

As my two kids progressed through public high school I launched numerous dinner table discussions with the same six words. Now that they've graduated, I'm going take one last crack at starting that way.

If I ran a high school...

...I'd make the demands of the school day fewer, and the school year longer. Kids don't have enough time to think straight let alone juggle classes, clubs, sports, homework and family, and still get 8 to 9 hours of sleep each night, which most experts believe is necessary. There is even research showing that teens have fewer accidents just getting to school if the bell rings later. At our local high school in Carmel, Calif., they considered starting classes an hour later, at 8:45 a.m., based on numerous studies showing teens don't function best at an earlier hour. The plan was scrapped when complaints poured in about the impact on after school sports activities.

Yet, the U.S. is falling behind, and a cue can be taken from nations that have a shorter summer break. More 10-day vacations rather than two or three months off would be better than the current American approach.

...I'd cut down on homework, particularly the busy-work kind, even in AP and honors classes. I'd also command teachers to coordinate tests so they don't pile up on the same days.

...Speaking of honors classes, I'd fix the problem some schools face with a "weighted" grade-point system that forces high achievers to opt out of electives - such as music or journalism - because even an "A" in those classes would lower their GPA.

...I'd give more time for a healthy lunch (our kids got 35 minutes). And I'd forbid clubs and other school groups from holding meetings at lunch, which serve to reduce meals to a few hasty bites.

...I'd see to it that all students in all grades have organized exercise daily, unless they play a team sport, in which case I'd place them in a special study hall where they can catch up on homework.

...I'd insist that loaded backpacks not be so heavy. The potential back strain won't necessarily show up for years, when it's too late. I see that a high school in Clearwater, Fla., is going to distribute Kindle e-readers to its 2,100 students, with all textbook content loaded on the single lightweight device.

...However, I'd prohibit cell phones and other personal communication devices in classes. It astonishes me that some teachers allow texting in the classroom.

...I'd stop kids who do poorly in class from "making up" the credits by taking virtually useless online courses run by outside companies.

...I'd be more conscientious about controlling the cost to each family for what is presumed to be a "free" public school education. If gym shorts cost $20, a yearbook $75, a field trip $170, an athlete fee $100, etc., then pretty soon free schooling isn't so free. The school board in Brooksville, Fla., just vetoed a music trip to Scotland for which each student was going to be charged $6,000.

...I'd require students in band and orchestra to wear earplugs. Studies have shown how high volume affects kids' hearing; one study even revealed that many music teachers suffer serious hearing loss without protection.

...I'd end the practice of allowing seniors to leave school early each day if they have sufficient credits for graduation. High school isn't college, and 12th graders should have the same length work day as every other student.

...Maybe I have a professional bias, but I'd see to it that every school library carries several daily newspapers. And no matter how much technology the library acquires, I'd insist that for the foreseeable future it also continues to have actual printed books.

...Finally, I'd seek to reduce the stress that comes with college applications and admissions. A four-year college education at an expensive, big-name institution isn't worth making a student an emotional wreck during four years of high school.

As it happens, I'm not an administrator or teacher or anyone responsible for implementing these changes. In fact, I'm no longer even a high school parent. So I'm leaving these notes with you, while I strike up a dinner conversation about what I'd do if I ran a college...

LOW FINANCE

The Coca-Cola Column

I'm calling this column Coca-Cola. Although I have little to say about Coke, it's my hope that the giant soft drink company will send me a few bucks for the naming rights.

Apparently during the current economic upheaval, names are the easiest things to pawn off. New York City got $4 million by allowing Barclays to put its name on a few subway stations. Ohio State University named its new student union after U.S. Bancorp in return for $1 million. Lansing, Mich., collected $1.5 million from a law school to name its minor-league baseball park Cooley Law School Stadium. The zoo in Columbia, S.C., desperate for cash, even auctioned off naming rights to a baby giraffe.

In one of the boldest naming ploys to date, the city of Topeka, Kansas, changed its name to Google for a month. Seems the deciders at Google were looking for a community in which to test ultra high-speed Internet service, and Topeka hoped to woo the business by adopting the Google name. Despite the flattering by Topeka, Google went elsewhere in Kansas.

What's next? Could taxpayers save some money if the nation's capital were renamed AIG, D.C.?

This form of crass commercialism isn't new. Every June, Dublin, Texas, changes its name to Dr. Pepper to commemorate the nation's first Dr. Pepper bottling facility located there. The town of Clark, Texas, changed its name to Dish, so that residents could all get free satellite TV.

Much of the blame for commercially motivated renaming goes to the town fathers in Derry Church, Pa., who in 1906 became so overwhelmed with gratitude for the success of the local chocolate factory that they renamed the town Hershey.

One hundred years later, Washington, Pa., temporarily renamed itself Steeler, Pa., when the NFL Steelers won the Super Bowl. Odder still was the decision by Ismay, Montana, in 1993 to officially change its name to Joe, Montana (after the star quarterback).

The concept isn't even new in Topeka, which prior to becoming Google had temporarily changed its name to ToPikachu after the Pokemon character.

Halfway, Ore., renamed itself Half.com in 1999, after the e-commerce site owned by eBay, in return for school computers and $100,000 cash.

Once upon a time companies didn't have to bother paying for naming rights, they simply picked a city they liked and commandeered the name. The famous fig cookie firm did that with Newton, Mass.; the GM people did it with Pontiac, Mich.

There are still plenty of existing towns to which American organizations might wish to relocate based on their unique names. There's Boring, Ore., which would probably be thrilled to become the site of new studios for NBC. There's Looneyville, Texas, which could house national headquarters for the Tea Party movement.

Why has the IRS overlooked the opportunity to relocate to Needmore, Texas? Shouldn't certain homophobic politicians be made to live in Gayville, South Dakota? A fitting home for the U.S. Congress would be Truth or Consequences, New Mexico.

If I'd had the time to relocate myself, I probably should have done my writing in Embarrass, Minnesota.

Fact is, all too many of us still hang our hats in Almighty Buckville, USA.

◆ ◆ ◆

Penny Wise

Congress has taken Herculean steps to protect the dollar, but I'd like to say a few words in defense of the penny.

It seems that in the midst of the nation's financial troubles there are some who believe being "penny wise" doesn't apply to pennies themselves. Editorial writers at the *Los Angeles Times* and *Chicago Tribune* are firmly on record as saying they believe pennies should be eliminated.

Due to the soaring price of zinc, the primary metal in modern pennies, the U.S. loses about $55 million a year making one-cent coins. That's why it's illegal to melt down pennies.

"The cent has outlived its usefulness," stated the Times. "Think of the penny as an old habit that doesn't work for us anymore."

Tell that to Ed Knowles of Flomation, Ala., who years ago began tossing his pennies in jars, and when those overflowed switched to oil drums. When he finally took the pennies—all 4.5 tons of them - over to the Escambia County Bank, he found he had saved $10,480 (and 13 cents).

Or, you could debate the penny controversy with residents of Fort Scott, Kan., who raised money for a park renovation project by laying 10 tons of pennies end-to-end. The resulting chain, over 40 miles long, set a Guinness record.

Those who pooh-pooh pennies make a big deal of the fact that nothing costs a penny anymore. Indeed, when visiting Massachusetts, "Good Morning America" host Robin Roberts expressed dismay that "penny candy" was being sold at Williams & Sons Country Store in Stockbridge for a dime!

But there are some compelling arguments for holding on to the Lincoln penny, first minted in 1909 as a replacement for the Indian head penny.

If the U.S. eliminated the one-cent coin, merchants would round up prices (you don't think they'd round down, do you?). By one estimate, that process alone would cost consumers about $100 million a year. Then, too, many charities would lose out on pennies that are collected at schools and retail stores. Americans seem more willing to hand over pennies to a good cause than to part with "real money."

Many of us have a nostalgic soft spot for pennies. When I was seven, my parents gave me a blue cardboard folder to collect pennies by year. I loved digging through whatever coins I could find—under the sofa or in my father's trousers—in search of pennies to fill my book.

As a teen I would bike to where the railroad came through town and carefully place a penny on the track. Then I'd wait, heart racing in anticipation, for a train to come by. If hit just right the penny would be squished to triple its size, creating a souvenir no longer usable in stores but quite valuable as proof of how close one had been to a speeding train.

I remember the odd habit some of our neighbors had each Halloween of distributing apples, each with a dozen or so pennies wedged inside. It left the coins sticky and wet, and pretty much spoiled a perfectly good apple, but it was exciting to receive.

To this day, no one in my family walks past a penny on the ground without stopping to pick it up. It's fiscal responsibility in its smallest measure. It's a good feeling. And it's good luck, right?

In February 2009, the first of four newly designed pennies was issued to mark the 200th anniversary of Abe Lincoln's birth, so the little coin that could seems safe for a while.

Government is wise to resist efforts to dump the penny. But that's not to say when conducting the nation's business it still wouldn't hurt to pinch a few.

◆◆◆

Struggling with Innumeracy

For most Americans, a penny at the gas pump has vivid significance but billions of dollars create a meaningless blur. Increasingly, we are unable to fathom the really big numbers in our modern world, a condition known as innumeracy.

In a 24-hour period while I was writing this, Facebook paid $1 billion for the photo-sharing service Instagram, which just a week earlier was valued at $500,000; Microsoft gave AOL more than $1 billion for some patents, and Sony said its annual loss was $6.4 billion.

Do these numbers mean anything anymore?

Not long ago people used the term "billion" so infrequently that, for clarity, they spelled the first letter: "That's billion, with a B." Now, according to *Forbes*, there are 1,226 billionaires.

Years ago, comedians mocked Carl Sagan because he talked about "billions of stars" as if it were, you know, an impressive number. Now, trillion is the new billion. And a million? Let's just say "Who Wants to Be a Millionaire?" doesn't titillate TV viewers—or bankers—the way it once did. Congress spends billions here, billions there and, as the late

Sen. Everett Dirksen famously concluded, "pretty soon you're talking about real money."

During the height of Mega Millions lottery fever, NBC News asked ticket buyers what they'd do with $650 million if they won. One woman said, with apparent sincerity, that she would purchase a life-time supply of Oreo cookies.

That's classic innumeracy. If the woman lives 60 more years, and is willing to eat 150 Oreos every week, her tab would be roughly $70,000. It's a lot of money, but as a percentage of $650 million it's so small—about one-hundredth of one percent—that, for all intents and purposes she could have her Oreos *and* $650 million.

Try getting a grip on numbers like these: Google's revenue is $25 billion a year! Matt Cain of the San Francisco Giants makes $3,000 per pitch! The U.S. government spends $1.5 million per minute!

Big numbers, right? Well, the real figures are actually double: Google is taking in $50 billion; Cain earns $6,000 every time he throws the ball, and the government's outflow is $3 million per minute. So what?

The mathematician and scholar Douglas Hofstadter coined the term innumeracy some 30 years ago, back when the national debt was under $2 trillion. It's climbed to eight times that, but the numbers are so large that an 800% increase has basically no meaning for average Americans, except that we know it's a lot of money.

What is a trillion, anyway? A trillion seconds ago, recorded human history had not begun. A trillion minutes ago, tool-making humanoids were emerging. A trillion hours ago, dinosaurs thrived and the Atlantic Ocean was forming. A trillion days ago, complex single-celled life was developing. And a trillion weeks ago, there was no planet Earth.

According to one estimate, just counting to a trillion takes over 190,000 years. If we paid off the debt at the rate of a dollar per second, we would get it done in roughly half a million years—without interest.

Many of our elected leaders seem to suffer from what might be called poli-innumeracy—the inability to control the numbers that control us. That's how we get bridges to nowhere and the military's infamous thousand-dollar toilet seats.

Other parts of the world have chosen to give their politicians more breathing room when it comes to talking about big numbers.

In Great Britain, France and Germany, for example, a billion has twice as many zeros as a million (bi); a trillion has three times as many zeros (tri). Thus, in Europe, an American trillion is called a billion. And a European trillion? We call that a quintillion—a number followed by 18 zeros.

It's only a matter of time before U.S. politicians start talking about a sextillion of this (21 zeros) or a vigintillion of that (63 zeros).

Travelers used to find it amusing to deal with foreign currencies that required, say, 10,000 whatevers for a cup of coffee. I remember visiting Brazil in the 1980s when taxi drivers needed a daily printout to determine how many thousand Cruzeiros to collect per mile.

These were "new" Cruzeiros, which differed from the "old" Cruzeiros in that the Brazilian government chopped off a few zeros so that one of the new was worth 1,000 of the old. A few years later they did it again, declaring that 1,000 new Cruzeiros would be worth one Cruzado. Soon they had to drop away three more zeros and Brazilians were given the "new" Cruzados. In 1990, these Cruzados Novos were retired, and the Cruzeiros were back; in 1993, the Cruzeiros lost another three zeros and were turned into "real" Cruzeiros. The numbers ceased to have meaning, although the value of the service or product remained clear.

What divides Americans nowadays is not just that a few people have a lot of money while many have much less, it's that some people understand the really big numbers—or so we assume—but most of us do not. Yet, as our innumeracy worsens, we don't trust bureaucrats who claim to understand huge sums. Too many of them seem to be clueless about the nation's budget, and also the price of an Oreo.

◆◆◆

HOLIDAY SPIRIT

Where Charity Begins

A radio commercial for the United Way makes a good point: Some people who have been contributors in past holiday seasons are now in need themselves.

An even more sobering reminder comes from the international relief organization Oxfam America: The season's must-have holiday gifts are food and water.

I thought about both messages while taking a phone call from a volunteer at our local high school with a polite request for a donation to support the baseball team. I wished her well but said that right now, with so many Americans out of work, homeless and hungry, every dollar I can spare will have to go to more urgent causes.

Was I wrong? At holiday time, when the bulk of the year's charitable giving occurs, perhaps we should apply a triage system in making our donations.

Americans give roughly $300 billion to charities each year, but only about 10% goes directly to social and human services, which includes food and shelter. More money goes to education, primarily colleges and universities. About a third is donated to churches and religious organizations, many of which, it should be noted, operate programs to help the hungry. Even so, a surprisingly small percentage of the nation's charitable giving winds up feeding and sheltering folks who desperately need it.

If you encountered a starving child holding a starving puppy, would your first step be to offer food to the dog? Obviously not. Yet we buy new uniforms for the baseball team, build a new wing on the college library, and give cash to our public radio station at a time when a Gallup poll shows that almost one in five Americans have struggled to feed themselves or their families one or more times per year—a rate three times higher than among people in China.

This correlates precisely with Census Bureau figures showing that over 20% of American children live in poverty. Among black children, the figure is a staggering 38%.

The nation's food banks are being squeezed badly, dealing with steep cuts in federal aid at the very time when the number of hungry people is expanding.

It's not as if Americans don't care, sometimes they just don't focus. When CBS's "60 Minutes" presented a moving close-up by Scott Pelley of homeless families in central Florida who have taken to living in their cars and trucks, and parking at gas stations to use the bathrooms, more than a million dollars came in, even though the broadcast made no request for donations.

On the other hand, there remains an unfortunate skepticism in the minds of some when it comes to funding human services. Recipients are gaming the system, it is argued, taking handouts instead of working harder. The nation's unemployment figures and statistics regarding hunger would seem to refute that—or at least render concerns about a few irrelevant, considering the needs of many.

Then, too, there are complexities in the mind-sets of donors. Some people are moved by causes that only interest them or have touched them directly. People give to schools they attended, fund research into diseases that affected loved ones and donate to churches as a direct expression of their faith.

Several representatives of charities not connected with human services told me that it's a mistake to assume that if donors didn't channel money to them it would necessarily go to other causes. More likely, it wouldn't be given away at all.

This may be the time to amend that, because the need for the basics of life are so urgently needed by so many.

Giving to any good cause is always better than not giving at all. Right now, giving to those who need it most is better yet.

◆ ◆ ◆

At Thanksgiving...

I'm thankful that many merchants are now considerate enough to begin Christmas sales shortly after Columbus Day, to avoid interfering with Halloween and Thanksgiving.

I'm also thankful that:

...Starbucks managed to put the snowflake designs on its paper cups long before most of the country got any snow.

...The Neiman Marcus Christmas Book—a catalog so lavish they call it a book—included a $15,000 edible gingerbread playhouse.

...Kids in North Attleboro, Mass., were spared the agony of waiting for Santa much beyond Halloween, as the *Sun Chronicle* reported, "The jolly old elf pulled up on a North Attleboro fire truck" on Nov. 5.

...Major retailers have the good sense to stagger their hours the day after Thanksgiving so we're not all lined up outside the same store at the same time. Why wait until 4 a.m. when there's a store opening at midnight or even at 8 or 9 the night before?

And, who among us isn't thankful that:

...CBS reporter Susan Koeppen was able to offer advice on how to "avoid the holiday mall madness." Among her tips: "Avoid crowds by shopping during stores' early and late extended hours."

...*The New York Times* dug up a helpful quote about holiday shopping from Melissa Geick, the manager of a Victoria's Secret store: "Just be prepared to face the music, and know that you're going to wait in line."

...Just in time for holiday buying, Walmart opened a store in Salinas, Calif., less than a mile from the city's other Walmart.

...*PC Magazine* asked and answered this pressing holiday question: "While you're standing in line with your cart, don't you get the nagging feeling you could do better somewhere else?" The solution, according to *PC*, is to use one of six "shopping apps" that allow you to check how much you're about to overpay while you're waiting to pay.

...Home Shopping Network demonstrated how delightful a Christmas tree looks with brightly wrapped gift bags of Huggable Hangers piled underneath. The pitch: "Spread some holiday tidiness! Wrap up and give a dozen hangers in the fun tote-style bag for the perfect instant gift. Add a Forever Fragrant holiday snowflake as a special touch. What better way to reign in the clutter and ring in the New Year?"

Plus, I'm especially thankful that:

...We now have websites such as Black-Friday.net, with investigative reporters uncovering stories like the one headlined, "Target 4-Day Pre-Black Friday Ad Leaked." And a website known as BlackFridayby-BradsDeals.com, which notified its readers, "Black Friday is not an official government holiday."

...The wildly successful online retailer known as Groupon.com had the bright idea to borrow unabashedly from the "Seinfeld" episode about "Festivus," and renamed the holiday season "Grouponicous."

...When it comes to holidays the general public is apparently no wiser than Congress. A Harris poll indicated that 69% of U.S. shoppers don't bother keeping to a budget when Christmas shopping.

Most of all, I'm thankful that for one day many of us manage to dodge the creeping commercialism and celebrate what is perhaps the best American holiday, when gifts are replaced by the simpler joys of gathering with family and friends to remember how fortunate and grateful we really are.

Happy Thanksgiving!

◆ ◆ ◆

Oh, by Golly

It was more than a month before Christmas when our local middle-of-the-road music station declared: "All Christmas, all the time!" And seconds later, "Holly Jolly Christmas" popped out of the car radio.

This wasn't the Lady Antebellum version released in late 2012; it was the 1965 original by the folk singer Burl Ives. Next came "White Christmas," but not the version Lady Gaga recorded; it was, of course, Bing Crosby's original—the largest-selling record of all time—released 70 years earlier.

In any year, Hollywood creates several hundred new films, networks churn out dozens of new TV series, and the music industry releases several thousand new songs. Yet when it comes to Christmas music, we dial up the same traditional melodies year after year. Curiously, the good old days for holiday pop music seem to have occurred during a 20-year stretch, beginning in the early 1940s.

Much of the American Christmas music tradition took root during World War II, a period that saw the release of "Holiday Inn" (1942), in which Crosby first sang Irving Berlin's heart-string tugging "White Christmas." It was a time when live music ruled the radio networks, giving prominence to pop-standard stars of the time, who recorded the songs that remain popular today as holiday classics. Soldiers far from home, and families awaiting their return, shared these tunes that stressed home, hearth and family. Back then, most people heard the same radio shows and saw the same movies. It was all a shared experience, quite unlike with today's fragmented media.

The war era was a golden age of holiday spirit, not only for Christmas music, but also for the holiday films still cherished at this time of year—"It's a Wonderful Life," multiple versions of "A Christmas Carol," "Miracle on 34th Street" and many etceteras. It was a time of relative innocence that many folks regard with a sense of deep nostalgia.

In the 1950s there was a burst of pop holiday creations, such as "Rockin' Around the Christmas Tree," "I Saw Mommy Kissing Santa Claus" and "Jingle Bell Rock." These too are staples on the 2012 holiday playlists.

It's hard to imagine that today anyone would write such a simplistic ditty as "Rudolph the Red-Nosed Reindeer," which first appeared in story form in 1939 as part of a printed promotion for Montgomery Ward department stores. Ten years later, songwriter Johnny Marks—who was also responsible for "Holly Jolly Christmas"—converted it to the tune that Gene Autry would record, selling two million copies in 1949. Today, it remains an indelible favorite, the second-biggest holiday hit behind "White Christmas."

Contemporary artists still record new holiday albums each year. Yet these contain almost exclusively tunes from the golden age. The 2012 release by the country-pop trio Lady Antebellum, for example, includes just one new song, the title track "On This Winter's Night," plus 11 covers of surefire favorites including "I'll Be Home for Christmas" (1943), "Have Yourself a Merry Little Christmas" (1943) and "Blue Christmas" (1948).

Rolling Stone asked its readers to pick the greatest Christmas song of all time, and they came up with the more than three-decades-old "Happy Xmas (War Is Over)" by John Lennon. The same year, 1979, Paul McCartney wrote and recorded "Wonderful Christmastime" which, according to Forbes, has earned him roughly $500,000 every year since.

Despite the potential payoff, newly composed holiday music is rare. Mariah Carey's 1994 release "All I Want for Christmas Is You" is one of the few monster holiday hits in recent decades. The song ranks highest among all digital downloads of Christmas music since 2003, but in second place is "The Chipmunk Song (Christmas Don't Be Late)" from 1958.

A generation that wouldn't recognize the cars, can't fathom the fashions, and might never buy other music of the 1940s is in the shopping malls again this season, humming along with Gene Autry. Would they ever imagine that he was known as "the singing cowboy" and often performed with a guitar on horseback?

Our special fondness for decades-old holiday music seems immune to forces that change almost everything else around us. Now that's a holly jolly thought.

◆ ◆ ◆

OUR LIVING LANGUAGE

Language Resolutions

Here's hoping that we're done naming colors "the new black." Gray worked as the new black for a while. And, sure, 2012's big Latino vote meant brown was the new black, but, really, making anything else the new black would be so, you know, random.

I'm wishin' that broadcasters will stop droppin' their g's. Linda Cohn of ESPN, I'm talkin' to you! No more goin' to the hoop and scorin'.

Politicians should resolve to never again say, "The American people want..." Are they claiming that every single American contacted them personally with a detailed explanation of his vote? Really? (And, Seth Meyers of SNL, thanks, but we're done with really.)

MSNBC folks, it's OK for the president, but the rest of us should quit sayin' "folks." More pressing: stop adding "sort of" to each sentence. That affect is spreading among progressives—especially on your show, Melissa Harris-Perry!—sort of every 30 seconds.

Mr. Blitzer, you and the others at CNN have to stop crying wolf—or, as you refer to it, "Breaking News!"

Now, Sean Hannity of Fox News Channel, you've fallen into a habit of starting sentences with "Now..." Check the tape.

Bob Schieffer of CBS, let me ask you this question. Why do you begin questions on "Face the Nation" by saying, "Let me ask you this question"?

Radio traffic reporters: Why the right-hand lane and the left-hand lane? There's no "hand" involved. Also, ask your perky colleague who does the weather to stop saying, "There's rain for your Thursday, but it should dry out on your Friday." Saying "your" doesn't make weather more personal.

Attention hosts on QVC and HSN, we get it: you have your own way of saying just about everything. But must you always refer to prices as "price points"? Why is a color a "coloration" and fabric a "fabrication"? Also, is it really necessary to hype sales by warning, "When they're gone they're gone"?

In the real fashion world, phrases change as fast as styles, so in a flash, terms like manthropology and Gangnam style became, you know, so Kelvin.

Diane Sawyer of ABC, nice try, but "As we come on the air tonight" just isn't up there with "And that's the way it is."

TV reporters, as you write your makeshift scripts in the future, please refrain from using the term makeshift.

Jon Stewart, your "Daily Show" is the funniest thing on TV. Time to drop the faux bleeps and the overworked f-bombs.

Basketball announcers, how did "score" become "score the basketball"? Baseball announcers, why is it that all of a sudden every pitcher is concerned about "arm slot"? Football announcers, just because Jon Gruden says "down and distance" when he means just one or the other, don't rush to copy him, and just because Chris Berman favors "come on, man" doesn't mean you have to obsess over it.

Ambassador Susan Rice: Sorry, but you officially own the term "talking points." Throw the phrase off the linguistic cliff.

Right after the 2012 election we began cleansing words like Romnesia, Obamalarky, and Romney Hood from the lexicon. However, Mister President, during your second term please gin up a new expression to replace "gin up."

Some annoying catch phrases take years to trickle down. So, at the end of the day, only guests on Sunday talk shows are left saying "at the end of the day." They should throw the phrase under the bus. Or, kick that can down the road.

Bottom line (although we're probably finished calling it that): say what's on your mind in the clearest way possible, but please, don't tell us there's no there there.

◆◆◆

Too Funny for Words

When my dad, Allen Funt, produced "Candid Microphone" back in the mid-1940s, he used a clever ruse to titillate listeners. A few times per show he'd edit out an innocent word or phrase and replace it with a recording of a sultry woman's voice saying, "Censored." Audiences always laughed at the thought that something dirty had been said, even though it hadn't.

When "Candid Camera" came to television, the female voice was replaced by a bleep and a graphic that flashed "Censored!" As my father and I learned over decades of production, ordinary folks don't really curse much in routine conversation—even when mildly agitated—but audiences love to think otherwise.

By the mid-1950s, TV's standards and practices people decided Dad's gimmick was an unacceptable deception. There would be no further censoring of clean words.

I thought about all this when CBS started broadcasting a show titled "$#*! My Dad Says," which the network insisted with a wink should be pronounced "Bleep My Dad Says." There is, of course, no mystery whatsoever about what the $-word stands for, because the show was based on a highly popular Twitter feed, using the real word, in which a clever guy named Justin Halpern quoted the humorous, often foul utterances of his father, Sam.

Bleeping is broadcasting's biggest deal. Even on basic cable, the new generation of "reality" shows like "Jersey Shore" bleep like crazy, as do infotainment series like "The Daily Show With Jon Stewart," where scripted curses take on an anti-establishment edge when bleeped in a contrived bit of post-production. For a while there was even a cable series about relationships titled "Who the (Bleep) Did I Marry?"—in which "bleep" wasn't subbing for any word in particular. The comedian Drew Carey developed a series that CBS intended to call "WTF!" Still winking, the network said this one stood for "Wow That's Funny!"

Although mainstream broadcasters won a battle against censorship when a federal appeals court struck down some elements of the Federal Communications Commission's restrictions on objectionable language, they've always been more driven by self-censorship than by the government-mandated kind. Eager to help are advertisers and watchdog groups, each appearing to take a tough stand on language while actually reveling in the double entendre.

For example, my father and I didn't run across many dirty words when recording everyday conversation, but we did find that people use the terms "God" and "Jesus" frequently—often in a gentle context, like "Oh, my God"—and this, it turned out, worried broadcasting executives even more than swearing. If someone said "Jesus" in a "Candid Camera" scene, CBS made us bleep it, leaving viewers to assume that a truly foul word had been spoken. And that seemed fine with CBS, because what mainstream TV likes best is the perception of naughtiness.

TV's often-hypocritical approach to censorship was given its grandest showcase back in 1972, when the comedian George Carlin first took note of "Seven Words You Can Never Say on Television." The bit was recreated on stage at the Kennedy Center a few years ago in a posthumous tribute to Carlin, but all the words were bleeped—not only for the PBS audience but for the theatergoers as well.

Many who saw the show believed the bleeped version played funnier. After all, when Bill Maher and his guests unleash a stream of nasty words on HBO, it's little more than barroom banter. But when Jon Stewart says the same words, knowing they'll be bleeped, it revs up the crowd while also seeming to challenge the censors.

In its censorship ruling, the appeals court concluded, "By prohibiting all 'patently offensive' references to sex ... without giving adequate guidance as to what 'patently offensive' means, the F.C.C. effectively chills speech, because broadcasters have no way of knowing what the F.C.C. will find offensive." That's quite reasonable—and totally beside the point. Most producers understand that when it comes to language, the sizzle has far more appeal than the steak. Broadcasters keep jousting with the F.C.C. begging not to be thrown in the briar patch of censorship, because that's really where they most want to be.

Jimmy Kimmel ran a segment on his late-night ABC program called "This Week in Unnecessary Censorship." He bleeped ordinary words in clips to make them seem obscene. How bleepin' dare he!

Censorship, it seems, remains one of the most entertaining things on television.

◆◆◆

Burn This Letter

D ear President Obama:
Here's a small piece of advice. But whatever you do, please don't cite this letter in your next speech.

In fact, Mister President, please don't mention any more letters. Ever. You're a powerful, articulate orator. I love listening to your speeches. But the "I've received a letter from..." thing just isn't working.

In your major speech about the budget mess, you said, "The other day I received a letter from a man in Florida. He started off by telling me he didn't vote for me and he hasn't always agreed with me." And then this unnamed guy went on to say it's a great country, and we're "lost in a quagmire of petty bickering," and blah, blah.

We know you receive hundreds if not thousands of letters each day. We know that you review a random sample of these each evening, which is good. And we assume that the letters reflect the sharp divisions in the country - which is to say you've probably got a letter handy to argue just about any point you're interested in advancing.

One Friday evening you spoke to the nation about the last-minute deal to avoid a government shutdown. You said, "A few days ago, I received a letter from a mother in Longmont, Colorado. Over the year, her son's eighth grade class saved up money and worked on projects so that next week they could take a class trip to Washington, D.C." This person urged you to get beyond "petty grievances and make things right." Sounds like a really solid citizen.

The problem with these letters is that they carry no weight and have modest credibility, especially nowadays when everyone uses e-mail to vent, fuss and opine. Your critics might suspect a trick, and people like Donald Trump will start ranting that the letters are fakes.

You probably recall the story told by William Safire, the renowned columnist who served as a speechwriter for one of your trickiest predecessors, Richard Nixon. Before important speeches, Safire would pop into the Oval Office and say, "Mr. President, I suggest you take the easy way out." Then, Nixon went on TV and read the speech Safire had written with the line, "Some in my administration have suggested I take the easy way out, but that would be wrong."

I don't think you're quoting phony communications; you're just using currency that has no value. Do we really care that a guy in Florida and a woman in Colorado advocate goodness?

In a national radio speech you said, "A few months ago, I received a letter from a woman named Brenda Breece." This woman, who lives in Missouri, wrote, "I watch the food budget ... We combine trips into town [and] use coupons ... and we trim each other's hair when we need a haircut."

You used the letter to underscore the fact that government needs to manage its money, just like Mrs. Breece and her family. Well, sure, we get it.

I recently received a letter that I sent to myself the other day that recalled how Gilda Radner made marvelous use of letters when playing Roseanne Roseannadanna on "Saturday Night Live." For example: "A Mr. Richard Feder from Fort Lee, New Jersey writes in and says: 'Dear Roseanne Roseannadanna, Last Thursday, I quit smokin'. Now, I'm depressed, I gained weight, my face broke out, I'm nauseous, I'm constipated, my feet swelled, my gums are bleedin', my sinuses are clogged, I got heartburn, I'm cranky and I have gas. What should I do?' ... Mr. Feder, you sound like a real attractive guy! ... You belong in New Jersey!"

If, Mister President, you do insist on quoting from my letter in your next speech, I'd like to close by saying, don't abandon your beliefs in what America stands for, don't give in to those who want only to help the rich get richer, stay the course, and, above all, don't raise the price of a First Class stamp.

◆◆◆

G Whiz

In one of his many speeches, President Obama said that without a new energy policy, "folks will keep on makin' conventional cars." Better vehicles already exist he said, adding, "we don't have to create somethin' new."

Golly g. Is the president makin' the trend, or just followin' it? It's hard to tell, but Americans really seem to be enjoyin' droppin' their g's.

George W. Bush was a famous g-dropper, always workin' hard at bein' a man of the people. Sarah Palin is a calculating leader of the no-g movement. She's constantly sayin' goin' and tryin' and wantin'. But when it comes to controversial political issues, Palin will usually revert to full g-force to tell us what's worth fighting for or voting for—with the g firmly in place.

Levying taxes, a serious matter on both sides of the aisle, is never spoken of as taxin'.

President Obama, too, seems able to shift from g-dropping to g-adding, depending on the nature of the audience or tone of his message. One clue: If the president uses the term "folks" in his speech, then it's almost certain that many words will be g-free.

Regardless, the official White House transcripts—as with the energy speech cited above—always include the g's, even in cases when they were never uttered by the president.

Women seem to have embraced g-dropping more than men. TV host Meredith Vieira often speaks about goin' somewhere or talkin' about something or sayin' this or that.

Funny how things are changin'. In his autobiography, Bill White, the acclaimed baseball player and broadcaster, explains that in the early 1970s he spent many hours with a voice coach trying to curb his habit of dropping g's in sports reports. If he were still on the air today, White would presumably need coaching to get rid of those g's he worked so hard to reinstate.

The absence of g's can be rather pleasant in conversation—even in presidential policy speeches—to a point. Personally, though, I find I pass that point when the pattern becomes obvious; when it's distracting. (Alas, having read this far, you are probably cursed to joinin' me.)

Linguists and social scientists who have examined the matter point out that the rate of g-dropping tends to be more prevalent among lower classes—but it also goes up among higher classes when striving for greater informality and lightheartedness.

In his linguistics class at the University of Pennsylvania, instructor Mark Liberman noted, "nearly all English speakers drop g's sometimes, but in a given speech community, the proportion varies systematically depending on formality, social class, sex, and other variables." After studying speeches by President Obama, Liberman observed, "Obama's dropped g's tend to occur in verb forms whose subjects are 'ordinary

Americans,' and whose meaning has something to do with the struggles of ordinary life."

So, when politicians and network anchors drop their g's, is it pandering? Meredith Vieira never misses a g when reading a news script, only when interviewing guests or chatting with her cohorts. President Obama didn't drop many g's in his State of the Union address, but was more comfortable doing so in his energy speech to college students.

The larger issue is verbal sloppiness. Casual communication is one thing, but the trend, possibly inspired by social networking, is to be quick and careless.

Here's hopin' the nation's most admired communicators don't overreach for the common touch—even when seekin' to connect with us regular folk.

Elegant speech is worth preserving. Just sayin'.

Ha!

I'd like to make a few observations regarding the word "ha."

Thanks to Chris Matthews, the engaging yet often bombastic host of "Hardball" on MSNBC, this laughable little term has popped into the media lexicon. Every time Matthews shouts "Ha!" his guests seem genuinely startled, much as they would if the host inadvertently let out a loud belch during the interview.

When former Governor Mike Huckabee said he was working on a list of rivals he'd like to make disappear, Matthews responded: "Ha!" When Virginia Republican Kate Obenshain confirmed she would never vote for a Democrat, Matthews replied: "Ha!" And when Barack Obama conceded he wasn't much of a bowler, Matthews knocked him over with a forceful: "Ha!"

Webster's New World says ha is, "an exclamation of wonder, surprise, anger, triumph, etc."—which covers quite a lot of territory.

Writers often use "ha, ha, ha" when alluding to a laugh, but genuine laughter can't really be written out, just as you can't spell the sound of a sneeze, which is why writers settle for "ah-choo." In fact, if you were to say the sounds "ha, ha" it would convey sarcasm—sort of like saying, "yeah, right."

On the other hand, you might say, "ah, ha." But that's not an expression of mirth, it's an announcement of discovery, best delivered emphatically: "Ah, ha!"

There is a sly dramatic laugh usually written, "heh, heh, heh." But that expression is most often used by cartoon characters.

Jackie Gleason, in his Ralph Kramden role, was fond of bellowing, "Har-har-hardy, har-har!" Alas, you don't hear that much anymore.

Whenever Santa Claus laughs, it's a jolly "ho, ho, ho." But as radio host Don Imus proved, a broadcaster can get in serious trouble if he misapplies "Ho!"

At first it was difficult to tell if letting out a "ha" was more a bodily function, like a yawn, but it's become clear that Matthews uses his pet utterance as a tool to punctuate conversation. For years whenever he said "ha!" it appeared in MSNBC's transcripts only as "(laughter)." Nowadays the transcripts actually say: "MATTHEWS: Ha!"

When Pennsylvania Rep. Jack Murtha was a guest, Matthews used it to cut him off in mid-sentence. That's when I realized he has perfected more than one "Ha!" There's the genuine-laugh "Ha!"; the fake-laugh "Ha!"; plus the wait-just-a-darn-minute "Ha!"—the one he used on Murtha.

I'm not suggesting Matthews has the social influence of, say, "Seinfeld," which taught many of us to say, "yada, yada, yada." But there's no arguing that we're hearing and reading "Ha!" with surprising frequency.

My daughter Stephanie, a law student who knows a bit about language, has taken to answering virtually all of my text messages with, "hahaha." Trouble is, I never know if she's ha-ha-ing with me, or at me.

◆ ◆ ◆

WE REALLY CARE ABOUT HAIR

Hair Today

Sure, Paul McCartney can still sing beyond age 70, but have you taken a good look at his hair? During the concert to benefit victims of Hurricane Sandy, and a few nights later on "Saturday Night Live," McCartney's locks were positively mesmerizing.

Madison Square Garden's gentle breezes made Sir Paul look like he and his hair were at a photo shoot for "Vogue." As a BBF (balding Beatles fan), I was torn between adoration and raging jealousy.

Most of us who attended the 1965 Shea Stadium concert are now gray and lucky to have any hair at all. Paul's mop, on the other hand, doesn't appear to have changed a bit.

And what about Mick Jagger? He bounded across the stage with his shoulder length hair looking thick and lustrous (a terrific hair word, but only for those who have plenty of it). Of course, Jagger's a

©Taylor Jones - El Nuevo Día   caglecartoons.com

full year younger than Paul.

I've seen famous folks with bad hairpieces, obvious dye jobs, and telltale transplants. But if Paul and Mick have had work done, it's mighty hard to tell. This is where the jealousy comes in. Many of us would take a second mortgage on our homes if we thought there was a foolproof way to add back realistic-looking hair.

As soon as the concert ended I Googled. Sure enough, the ever-vigilant British tabloids had more versions of the story than Alan Brady had toupees on the "Dick Van Dyke Show."

A headline last year in the *Daily Mail* asked, "Had a little Help! Sir Paul?" The report said McCartney had been "sporting a much thicker hairdo of late, reminiscent of his luscious lock worn while in The Beatles." A spokesman for Paul told the paper that speculation about hair weaves was "total rubbish" (a fine British term for things that are false or, on the other hand, might be true).

The Daily Mirror dug deep into the follicles of British scalp trends under the headline, "The bald truth behind celebrity hair transplants." Seems quite a few Brits invest in dramatic and expensive hair jobs. But the *Mirror* had no dirt on the state of McCartney's or Jagger's heads.

There was, however, a detailed analysis of Jagger's health habits in the *Daily Mail*, disclosing that Sir Mick is particularly fond of La Prairie's caviar skin cream from Switzerland, and the miraculous Crème de la Mer, which sells for $1,900 per pot (a proper British term for a 16.5-ounce jar).

Jagger's regime is also said to involve "lashings of hair dye" by an in-home technician, the result of Mick's "having exhaustively re-searched hair colouring and its application."

Well, now we're getting somewhere. At least there's evidence—if that's what you call the work of a British tabloid—that Jagger's getting some help up top. Both he and Paul seem to have auburn highlights that really must come from a bottle or pot.

Paul's voice is thinning with age, while his hair remains frozen in time. Wouldn't it be nice if science could flip that around?

By the end of the Sandy concert I decided I was more of a Billy Joel fan than I had realized. Joel, a mere 63 at the time, had gained a few pounds and lost most of his hair—and what remains on his dome is appropriately gray. He also refrains from bouncing around the stage (leaving us to wonder if he even can). He's a real New Yorker, a survivor in the manner of Billy Crystal and Matt Lauer, who also make do with pretty much whatever hair they have at the moment.

Oh, who am I kidding? These three guys probably look at Paul and double over in envy. (I'm sure they'd prefer to comb over in envy, if they had enough hair to do it.)

◆ ◆ ◆

Heads Up in Politics

Every four years, when politicians fight for the nation's top job, the selection ultimately hinges on one factor that always tips presidential elections. The race is won by a hair.

For over half a century, voters have unfailingly elected the candidate with the best hair—the guy with the lock on locks.

John Kennedy defeated Richard Nixon by a razor-thin margin in 1960. Nixon's already-receding, slicked-back 'do was no match for the young, wavy head of hair from Massachusetts.

After JFK's death, Democrats were stuck with Lyndon Johnson's lousy haircut and most certainly would have surrendered the White House had Republicans come up with any hairdo better than Barry Goldwater's. LBJ sealed victory by wearing a large cowboy hat whenever possible.

The nation soon plunged into a period of fallow follicles. Nixon re-emerged, beating perhaps the only two Democrats with weaker hair: Hubert Humphrey, whose receding hairline was made worse by a round face and prominent, barren forehead; and George McGovern, whose heart was in the right place but whose head was burdened with a horrid comb-over.

Vowing not to repeat the McGovern debacle, Democrats nominated the nation's most commanding haircut in Jimmy Carter. Republicans were powerless with the head of Gerald Ford, who by 1976 had lost most of the hair that helped him get to Washington in the first place.

Four years later, desperate Republicans turned to Hollywood for a candidate with a star-powered coiffure. Ronald Reagan trimmed Carter's chances and later won re-election by buzzing right through Walter Mondale's skimpy gray lid.

In 1988, many pundits were convinced that Michael Dukakis had the hair to beat George H.W. Bush. But voters thought the Dukakis 'do was too rigid, too perfect, too large for his smallish head. Rumors even swirled that he had a toupee. In the closing stages of the campaign Mr. Dukakis covered up with an army helmet but lost.

Bill Clinton ushered in a new wave of hair. Strangely appealing, especially to women voters, Mr. Clinton's flowing salt and pepper beat Mr. Bush, then overpowered Bob "this is my natural color" Dole.

By paving the way for executive gray, Clinton may have handed the 2000 election to George W. Bush, who managed to attract the "young gray" vote, though Al Gore was a hair's breadth away. John Kerry had overwhelming hair, but it wasn't enough to topple an incumbent head of state.

In 2008, America elected its first African-American haircut, as Barack Obama was pitted against the aging, outdated lid of John McCain.

The 2008 campaign also saw the emergence of strong female candidates including Hillary Clinton and Sarah Palin. It remains to be seen if Americans are too sexist to entrust their highest office to someone capable of having bad hair days, or to be caught in curlers when the red phone rings at 3 a.m.

An indication of how desperately the GOP wanted the White House in 2012 came when it briefly considered Donald Trump, an empty haircut if ever there was one.

What worried Democrats was that President Obama had been graying fast in office, while Republicans turned to one of the party's most dominant hairdos in Mitt Romney.

How will it all comb out in 2016? It's too early to tell, but while you waste time with Gallup and Pew, I'll be watching the barber poll.

◆◆◆

Media Split Hairs

Readers who saw my presidential hair column when it appeared in *The Wall Street Journal* were hopefully amused by my treatise: the winner in presidential elections is often the guy with the best haircut.

However, those who saw me doing this same "hair piece" on the Fox News Channel must have assumed I was some kind of crazed political scientist.

Then again, anyone whose source was MSNBC or the blogosphere must have taken me to be a right-wing loon who seriously believes the road to the presidency has something to do with hair follicles.

In media these days, the filter through which we evaluate news and information—especially on cable-TV and the Internet—is so clouded by bias that the content is becoming dangerously devalued.

The Journal column was a political parody, based upon a few snippets of historical fact. The "trend," I opined, began when John Kennedy defeated Richard Nixon by a hair; Nixon with a receding hairline and JFK with fabulous locks. Over the years, there was Jimmy Carter's dynamic 'do followed by Ronald Reagan's Hollywood-perfect haircut and by 2012 we had a pair of Republicans, Perry and Romney, with some of the hottest hair ever.

Fox News, which like the *Journal* is owned by Rupert Murdoch's News Corp., asked if I'd talk about the column on the morning program "Fox & Friends." I've been on that show before when I had something to plug, and it seemed harmless enough.

In fact, while I personally disagree with the political views of Fox News and most of its hosts, they seem perfectly capable of doing satire. All the morning shows—from "Fox & Friends" to "Today"—are eclectic mixes of hard news and fluff.

As I was introduced, host Juliet Huddy told viewers, "I swear to you, this is a scientific study." I immediately said, "Juliet, this couldn't be any *less* scientific."

For the next three minutes I rattled off quips about "health care versus hair care," and how Republicans might have done better in '08 with Romney's full head of hair rather than John McCain's graying wisps.

A few hours later, the blog Media-ite blared, "Fox & Friends: Candidates With The Best Hair Always Win Presidential Elections." In a particularly strange summary, the reporter said I was being "lighthearted" but also "seemed to be (speaking) seriously."

This hot news was picked up by MSNBC's Ed Schultz, who alerted viewers to the fact that, "This morning 'Fox & Friends' actually spent three minutes on a segment that suggested the candidate with the best hair always wins the White House."

Meanwhile, *The Atlantic* magazine's website selected the *Journal* column as one of the day's five best. Go figure.

Why have Fox News and MSNBC—owned by two of the world's largest news organizations—allowed themselves to become so obsessed with what the other is saying, particularly whenever it seems to confirm political prejudices? How can viewers of either outlet take seriously the ranting about the other?

And which is a greater waste of time: a three-minute satire about hair? Or criticism about doing such a satire?

The behavior of much modern media is a sad reflection of the new politics that is wrecking our country. Everything is black or white, left or right, and absolute. There's no room for compromise, and no tolerance for anything beyond the borders of rigid ideology.

I have no idea if the candidate with the best haircut will win. I do know that if media lose perspective—along with a sense of humor—we'll all get clipped.

◆ ◆ ◆

WHEELS OF GOVERNMENT

Taking Exception

Even in the midst of serious shortfalls involving the economy, education, health care, and military entanglements overseas, America remains truly exceptional in many ways. However, clinging to the phrase "American exceptionalism," and elevating it as yet another password for patriotism, only misappropriates the concept.

"They've refused to talk about American exceptionalism," said House Speaker John Boehner on CNN, referring to President Obama specifically and Democrats in general.

Asked why, Boehner offered: "I don't know. I don't know. I don't know if they're afraid of it, whether they don't believe it. I don't know."

The term American exceptionalism has evolved over nearly two centuries from what was once a way of defining the nation's origins and founding principles, to what many fear is now just code for jingoism. When used in drawing international comparisons, exceptionalism may simply mean "different." Used in domestic political contexts it usually means "better."

In one State of the Union message, President Obama alluded to the uniqueness of the U.S. "We are the first nation to be founded for the sake of an idea," he declared, "the idea that each of us deserves the chance to shape our own destiny." He called the U.S., "not just a place on a map, but the light to the world."

However, the president's failure to invoke the actual phrase "American exceptionalism" was enough to trigger Boehner's ire. Sarah Palin, in her latest book, is even more emphatic, stating bluntly that the president "doesn't believe in American exceptionalism at all." She writes, "He seems to think it is just a kind of irrational prejudice in favor of our way of life. To me, that is appalling."

As defined by the president's conservative critics, the concept of exceptionalism promotes the view that America is uniquely qualified to serve as an arbiter in global conflicts. It suggests that Americans are inherently superior, and that the nation's failures can be dismissed or rationalized merely by invoking a catch phrase.

Delivering the unofficial Tea Party response to the State of the Union, Rep. Michele Bachmann of Minnesota emphasized her belief in "the exceptionalism of America." She added, "I believe America is the indispensable nation."

These conservative challenges date back to remarks the president made in London in 2009, in which he outlined America's strengths and values, which, he concluded, "though imperfect, are exceptional." The president said he saw "no contradiction" between believing that the U.S. has "an extraordinary role in leading the world" and recognizing that "we can't solve these problems alone."

In his book, "The Limits of Power: The End of American Exceptionalism," Andrew Bacevich of Boston University argues it is an "ethic of self-gratification" that threatens the foundation of U.S. exceptionalism. He summarizes, "As the prerequisites of the American way of life have grown, they have outstripped the means available to satisfy them."

These prerequisites, as Bacevich calls them, help create the modern condition in which American exceptionalism, in a material sense, fosters anti-Americanism in many parts of the world.

Kathleen Parker, a CNN host at the time she questioned John Boehner about the word "exceptionalism," predicted, "We're going to be hearing it a lot in the coming months as Republicans try to out-exceptionalize each other for the presidential nomination."

A modest affirmation of America's exceptional qualities should not require a slogan, just as patriotism should not require a lapel pin, and religious conviction ought not be measured by the frequency of visits to church.

The nation is, as President Obama noted, both imperfect and exceptional. To dwell on phrases rather than principles only serves to underscore the imperfections.

◆◆◆

In God We Vote

The selection of Mitt Romney as the GOP's presidential nominee, along with Jon Huntsman's early success in the race, made certain that the 2012 campaign continued the trend of carefully weighing candidates' religious beliefs.

Both men were scrutinized because of their affiliation with the Church of Jesus Christ of Latter-Day Saints and, in Romney's case, because he had made religion a cornerstone of his previous campaigns. When he sought the presidency four years earlier, Romney famously said, "Freedom requires religion just as religion requires freedom."

But even without the focus on the two Mormon hopefuls, the need for national candidates to establish religious credentials is growing. With each election cycle, it is becoming increasingly important for politicians to pledge their faith in faith.

Basically, we're entitled to know everything about candidates for high office—right down to whether Coca-Cola is their preferred soft drink, as Tim Pawlenty eagerly confirmed; whether they have a valid birth certificate, and whether they've circulated lewd photos of themselves on Twitter.

Religious views are worth examining, we're told, insofar as they might influence a candidate's decisions. But is that relevant? Let's say candidate A favors a woman's right to have an abortion, while candidate B states that abortion violates his religious principles. Does it matter where the position originates?

A position is a position, regardless of how it's formed. However, yielding to pressure from religious organizations is something different, and certainly cause for concern.

Evaluating the Mormon candidacies, Paul Mero of the Sutherland Institute, a conservative think tank in Utah, wrote, "I, like many Americans, care that our nation's highest leader is a person of faith. It matters to me because it becomes a point of commonality and a measuring stick for me as to how I might better understand that person's politics and policies."

That's where the religious litmus test comes in. Many of the declared or potential candidates appear in Washington at "strategy briefings" sponsored by the Faith & Freedom Coalition, an organization headed by Ralph Reed of the Christian Coalition. They gather to state their support of the group's positions on issues such as abortion and same-sex marriage.

Back in 2008, as the campaign heated up, candidates appeared in a televised religious examination conducted by Rev. Rick Warren, author of "The Purpose-Driven Life." Among Warren's questions to Barack Obama and John McCain: What does it mean to you to be a follower of Jesus Christ?

Both men were guarded but answered dutifully. One wonders, however, if the reply, "I'm not a follower," would have meant instant disqualification—especially among Republicans, where Christianity has the strongest grip.

In the last three presidential elections, voters who identified themselves as "Protestant" or "other Christian," voted overwhelmingly for the Republican. Jews voted by large margins for the Democrat, as did those who said they were "unaffiliated" with any organized religion.

In a Quinnipiac poll, only 45 percent of Republicans surveyed said they had a "favorable" opinion of the Mormon Church.

Romney spoke of the matter at great length in his campaign four years earlier. "There are some who would have a presidential candidate describe and explain his church's distinctive doctrines," he said. "To do so would enable the very religious test the founders prohibited in the Constitution. No candidate should become the spokesman for his faith."

Yet, Romney's insistence that "freedom requires religion," diffused his argument—particularly for those who have witnessed the religious-cloaked turmoil in many parts of the world, as well as among those with no religious beliefs.

Those worried about the increasing role of religion in politics took note of the event staged by Texas Gov. Rick Perry, a possible Republican presidential candidate, which he called a "day of prayer," with a strictly evangelical Christian theme. Perry said he was seeking "spiritual solutions" to the nation's problems.

Many politicians pay lip service to separation of church and state, while kowtowing to powerful religious groups and bending over to answer questions about religion that really should have no part in the election process.

"It is apparently necessary for me to state once again not what kind of church I believe in—for that should be important only to me— but what kind of America I believe in." So said John F. Kennedy, as he sought to become the nation's first Catholic president.

Clearly, JFK would not have imagined, nor favored, the intense role that religion plays in presidential politics more than five decades later.

◆◆◆

Tuned Out

WASHINGTON—I decided to spend some time in the visitors' galleries on Capitol Hill, to see firsthand what political gridlock looks like.

On the Senate floor, Sherrod Brown, D-Ohio, was delivering a passionate speech about interest rates on student loans. "I just pray and beg my colleagues," he said, "please pass this. Keep student loan rates manageable."

When he finished the chamber fell silent. Why? Because none of Brown's colleagues was present. He was addressing 99 empty chairs.

Sparse attendance in Congress is an historical fact, but this scene was depressing nonetheless. The situation has gradually worsened as television and the Internet make it easier for members to stay in touch without actually setting foot in the chambers.

On the House side, Budget Committee chairman, Paul Ryan, R-Wis., was engaged in his favorite pursuit: slashing. "We're eliminating government slush funds to stop bailouts," he said of the GOP plan, "we're controlling runaway, unchecked spending."

It was hard to tell if the few dozen House members in attendance were listening to Ryan because most were busy with their own favorite pursuits: tapping away on iPads and smartphones.

One of the first things Rep. John Boehner, R-Ohio, did after becoming Speaker was revise House policy to permit mobile devices on the floor. The new rule allows electronics unless their use "impairs decorum," but policymakers stopped short of adding a requirement for House members to actually pay attention.

The day I was there a glitch in the system blocked Apple products—iPhones and iPads—connected to the official House network from receiving emails. This caused quite a fuss, with the newspaper *Roll Call* quoting a Democratic spokesman as saying, "Members of Congress have become more and more reliant on mobile technology for floor proceedings."

Is that a good thing? Congress has an approval rating of less than 15 percent, so you'd think avoiding distractions and showing up more often would be good first steps in improving public perception if not the actual legislative box score.

But the public doesn't get a clear picture of this on television. C-SPAN, the non-profit cable service providing coverage from the Hill, uses video feeds supplied by House and Senate TV departments—and they avoid showing vast expanses of empty seats or members distracted by handheld gadgets.

House rules require head-on coverage of members at the podium and forbid reaction shots inside the chamber. As a result, according to C-SPAN's chief Brian Lamb, the public gets "a less-than-complete view." In a letter to Speaker Boehner, Lamb called for a better "journalistic product" by allowing additional robotic cameras that would be controlled by C-SPAN's staff. Boehner, like Democrat Nancy Pelosi before him, said no.

One exception comes during the annual State of the Union speech, when television networks are allowed to determine the coverage. That yielded an infamous screenshot a few years back of Rep. Eric Cantor, R-Va., fiddling with his Blackberry during the president's speech. Cantor said he was taking notes.

I came away from my visit feeling like I had just been in a college lecture hall where the twin plagues are poor attendance by some, and relentless use of mobile devices by others.

I contacted a C-SPAN executive for an update on efforts to improve coverage, and was told that the service has now added High Definition. So? "Even with our limited range, if you look closely," the gentleman said, "you can see which members are using cellphones."

As more voters get HD, approval ratings for Congress might disappear entirely.

◆◆◆

Keep SCOTUS In Camera, Not on It

Whenever high-profile cases are heard by the U.S. Supreme Court—from the Affordable Care Act (Obamacare) to gay marriage—public interest soars. On such occasions, lifting the curtain on the workings of the nation's highest court would make spectacular television. But placing cameras in the court is a bad idea.

Television, as those of us who have worked in it know well, is a valuable tool but not a neutral observer. The very act of pointing a camera is an editing process that grows more subjective each time a director switches from one angle to another, or decides when to cut to a reaction shot. Rules governing coverage can address that, as with C-SPAN's telecasts of Congress, but such rules also tend to reshape the message into a TV version of "reality."

People usually behave differently when they know they are on television. Moreover, perception of on-screen images is not always the same as the view formed when content is evaluated without video.

Just look at what television has done to the nation's political debates. Way back in the first Kennedy-Nixon contest there was widespread belief that Nixon won the radio and print coverage, while Kennedy prevailed on TV. Kennedy looked tan and fit, while Nixon declined to wear makeup, affecting not only his appearance but also public reaction to his arguments. Should Chief Justice Roberts wear makeup to ensure that his comments are received in the best light?

TV helped presidential debates devolve to the spectacles they are today. Yet, despite television's power to influence and distort, televised debates are essential in the election process because the public requires information to pass judgment; the trade-off is acceptable.

Equally appropriate is C-SPAN's chronicle of Capitol Hill, although it, too, is flawed. The coverage is compromised by rules allowing members to speak to near-empty chambers while cameras avoid showing vacant seats or the bored reaction of colleagues.

Televised Congressional hearings are marked by grandstanding and politicking for the cameras, forcing more substantive discussions to be held behind closed doors. It's not entirely coincidence that Congress has become gradually less effective during the TV era.

The legal system, at least at the Supreme Court level, is not ready for such pressure or compromise.

Television's most infamous courtroom exercise, O.J. Simpson's murder trial in 1995, gave a national audience a lesson about the impact of TV. Most key participants played to the cameras, some overtly, and the entire production, right down to the verdict, made a mockery of the system.

My own experience in a televised trial—concerning, of all things, the appropriate behavior of hidden-camera TV—convinced me of the unintended consequences that came with coverage by Court TV. It was telling that when the judge ordered cameras turned off during one sensitive portion of the trial, a shift in demeanor was immediately apparent among attorneys, witnesses and even jurors.

Yet, powerful voices now advocate TV coverage of the Supreme Court. Justice Elena Kagan, the court's newest and youngest member, has stated that cameras would "make people feel so good about this branch of government." Indeed, most who favor the move tend to focus on the interest of the public rather than the impact on the process. Perhaps advocates are more familiar with law than with television.

Many point out that the court's public sessions are already available on audio feeds and in written transcripts—so what's wrong with broadening coverage to include video? The real question is why? If the full content is already available, what do TV viewers hope to learn? What the attorneys are wearing? How nervous they appear to be?

This is an age when many of our respected institutions are being subjected to increasingly irreverent behavior—much of it either provoked by, or widely distributed by, television. The Supreme Court must operate on a higher plane to preserve the dignity of its process and the integrity of its decisions. It should be spared the burden of TV's reality.

◆◆◆

Striking a Presidential Pose

Smile, you're the most powerful person on earth.

Only 43 men have posed for an official presidential portrait or photo. What ran through their minds? I must have a stern expression to convey authority? If I smile do I risk appearing smug? I don't want folks to see my crooked teeth?

The official photo in 2013.

In the 2013 official White House second-term photo, President Obama flashes a wide smile. There hasn't been anything like it since 1977 when Jimmy Carter established what stood for decades as the record for the toothiest presidential grin.

Looking at the gallery of White House images, we see that no president, not one, dared to crack even a slight smile until Gerald Ford revealed a few front teeth in his 1974 photo. It looked more like a smirk than a smile, and considering how Ford's presidency came about, maybe it was. Regardless, it established a trend in which all presidents smiled for the camera—until 2009.

Barack Obama, despite his mighty incisors, broke the chain of smiles in his first term photo, electing to go with a rather somber expression. Then, for his second term: Pow! The president is smiling broadly.

Although vice presidential smiles don't count for much, the Obama-Biden pairing has more dental sparkle than any administration in history. Of course, President Obama seems to flash his ultra-engaging smile at just the right moments, while Mr. Biden sometimes seems unable to rein his in, as was proved in last fall's vice presidential debate.

Like most things presidential, the question of how a Commander-in-Chief should look in his official portrait began with George Washington. It's often said that Washington had false teeth made of wood, making smiling difficult. That's only half true; he did have false teeth, but they were made of ivory and other expensive materials. Yet he did find smiling problematic because, according to numerous historians, his false teeth were spring-loaded, and he feared that if he cracked a smile his mouth might fly open.

You'll never see a picture of John Adams smiling, because he lost all his teeth and refused to wear false ones. Abe Lincoln was also beset by dental woes, having had his jaw broken as a dentist pulled one of his teeth. Jimmy Carter's mother, Lillian, once told a reporter that her son had "perfect teeth." She added that he was, occasionally, "overzealous about flossing."

In modern times, presidents pose for an official White House photo while in office, and then after leaving office authorize an official oil painting, for which they have an opportunity to reconsider their pose and facial expression. Jimmy Carter's portrait shows none of the teeth that flash in his official photo. Richard Nixon seems a bit more cheerful in his portrait than he ever did in office. George W. Bush is smiling in both images, but in his portrait removes his jacket, making him the only U.S. chief executive whose official portrait shows him in shirtsleeves.

Barack Obama is the first president to have his official photo taken with a digital

The 2009 version.

camera. According to experts it shows some evidence of being Photo-shopped to improve the lighting.

As Mr. Obama began his second term, he seemed to have planted clues in his two official photos to keep historians guessing. Was his somber expression in 2009 an indication of uncertainty in the job? Did he feel overwhelmed by the weight of history, as he became the first black president?

Why the big smile in 2013? Is the president still giddy over his surprisingly wide re-election margin? Is he sending a message to opponents in Congress that, like the banks, he's now too big to fail? And four years hence, which way will the Obama oil painting go: serious expression, or 1,000-watt smile?

It's too bad the administration didn't follow up on the suggestion to mint one of those trillion-dollar coins and put Mr. Obama's picture on it. Would he frown at the size of the national debt? Or, with great confidence, would he smile all the way to the bank?

SOCIAL MEDIA MADNESS

Our Disposable Culture

Much is written about the fact that denizens of social media often fixate on the moment. Texts and tweets fly across the street, the room, the aisle, conveying thoughts with half-lives measured in seconds. But dwelling in the present is one thing. To treat the present as disposable—so that, in effect, we gradually shrink our past—is something else.

With the mobile app known as Snapchat, users now exchange more than 60 million photographs each day. The primary appeal for the service's avid fans, who tend to be in their late teens, is that the images are never saved. The goofy poses, the silly jokes, even the loving glances—they all vanish within seconds. Life, at least as glimpsed through Snapchat, is entirely disposable.

Facebook was quick to launch a similar service that it calls Poke. It seems geared for those who worry that the regular Facebook, itself a flawed replacement for the trusted family album, is too permanent, too meaningful a repository for our thoughts and images.

One of Snapchat's slogans is "There is value in the ephemeral." Roughly translated: There is no point in taking good photos, or worrying about your appearance, or fretting over bad behavior, because it's all going to disappear quickly, only to be replaced by the next batch of evanescence. Life is a blur and leaves no traces.

Not surprisingly, Snapchat and Poke have also become popular for sexting, one type of communication where lasting memories can do more harm than good.

Yet it isn't just teens who seem to have devalued the past. Appearing on NBC's "Today" show, Barbara Reich, a self-described expert on combating clutter, practically brought her interviewer, Willie Geist, to tears when he asked Ms. Reich about saving and preserving his young daughter's artwork. "What if she makes something special and I want to put it up on the wall?" Mr. Geist asked. "It's not really that special," she said. Get over it.

Ms. Reich, it turns out, is just as concerned with uncluttering our memory banks as she is with emptying our closets. She assured Mr. Geist that in years to come he'd never regret having chucked his daughter's art.

I find this jarring, because I treasure the projects that my kids made in school, just as I look back fondly on the photos of them growing up. We hear occasionally of people who are forced to flee when fire or flood threatens their home, and the one thing they clutch as they head out the door is the family album.

The great contradiction in the digital age is that while material is said to last indefinitely, its intangible quality may actually make it less permanent in our lives. When letters were written by hand, for example, some were saved and treasured. Is there much chance that anyone's emails will be preserved for posterity?

It's hard to imagine that electronic files of photos and even family videos will ever be passed down in digital form the way hard copies have always been. With popular online services such as Pandora, music is random and temporary: It comes and goes but isn't saved.

A new generation treats things differently, even tangible items like clothing. I still have a few fine garments that my father used to own, and my wife, Amy, takes pride in making beautiful pieces that can be saved and handed down. Nowadays, though, stores like Forever 21 and H&M are the rage because they offer what is known as disposable fashion. The garments are made so poorly and priced so inexpensively that they are often thrown away after a few wearings.

Nothing viewed only in the context of the moment—a photo, a child's drawing, an item of clothing—is as meaningful or instructive as something viewed over time in the context of history and our experiences.

We don't even seem to value truth as much as we used to— whether in government, the news media or relationships. It's all so fleeting. The big picture, it seems, has been shattered into countless smaller pictures, so easily deleted.

◆◆◆

Lindsey, Stoned and Pilloried

During a trip to Washington, D.C., a woman named Lindsey Stone posed for a snapshot while making crude gestures. She posted it on Facebook, and soon her life turned upside down.

The incident—and to even call it that is part of the story—serves to underscore the power of social media. Moreover, it exposes the extent to which mainstream media have become obsessed with whatever is echoing online.

Stone, 30, and a co-worker visited Arlington National Cemetery, where they noticed a small sign near the Tomb of the Unknown Soldier advising "Silence and Respect." As Stone had done earlier on the trip when she posed with a cigarette in front of a No Smoking sign, she mocked the cemetery advisory by opening her mouth as if yelling and raised her middle finger to convey disrespect. The behavior was juvenile, and posting the photo on Facebook was offensive, but what happened next was unexpected.

Protests about the snapshot erupted online, followed by a Facebook page devoted to getting Stone fired from her job at an assisted living facility in Massachusetts. Her employer responded by suspending Stone and her friend without pay. The Internet went into overdrive. Finally, WRC-TV in Washington reported the story, after which NBC's "Today" show devoted an entire segment to vilifying the two women.

Immediately following the network report the "Fire Lindsey Stone" site tripled its "likes." Hours later, Stone's boss made her dismissal permanent, despite her apology about the photo.

Stone wrote on Facebook that she "meant no disrespect to people that serve or have served our country," explaining that she was "challenging authority in general."

Perhaps she's naïve as well as impudent. But even in an era marked by intemperate social and political debate, the content on the "Fire Lindsey Stone" website is chilling. In addition to calling the woman every vile name possible, posters had published her phone number and address, along with those of her employer.

NBC's decision to run the story, especially the way it did, is even more troubling—the media equivalent of throwing gasoline on a fire.

"It's sad," "it's horrible," "what's happening to this world?" said the three anonymous people "Today" chose to broadcast. They weren't talking about the Internet or media; they were referring to Stone's offending photo. There was also the VFW member "Today" found in Hyannis, Mass., offering the comment, "Pretty disrespectful and stupid."

NBC's Natalie Morales concluded her report by predicting, "I think she's not going to be having a job after this." Is Morales siding with the Facebook mob that believes Stone deserved to be fired? The four "Today" hosts discussing the story seemed only to be concerned with the photo, not the violation of the woman's right to free speech, or the slander being heaped upon her online.

"Today" and its network counterparts report daily on what's "trending" in social media. Cable channels, too, are quick to run photos from Twitter—such as those during Hurricane Sandy—without checking their authenticity. These channels also run Tweets and Internet postings at the bottom of the screen, without knowledge of who the sender might be.

The result of all this is that mainstream media are gradually becoming tools of social media.

Lindsey Stone shouldn't have lost her job. Nor should she be subjected to the barrage of hate that has erupted over her warped idea of what's funny, and her misguided decision to post a photo of it online.

For their part, "Today" and other mass media must reassess the difference between shedding light and lighting a fire.

Got Apps?

Even if you don't own a single app—and these days that hardly seems possible—you had to be taken aback when Yahoo decided to pay a British teenager $30 million for an app called Summly.

Nick D'Aloisio, 17, said the idea came to him because he was looking for a way to skim through lengthy articles (read that "homework") so he built an app that basically summarizes lengthy documents into 400 characters. Now all he needs is an app that simulates laughing all the way to the bank.

There seems to be no limit to folks' fascination with apps that simulate the sound of bubble wrap or—a real favorite—flatulence.

A guy was showing me the new apps on his iPhone. He seemed unable to put down the device, even for a moment, preferring to poke away with both thumbs while explaining the process.

He said one app could show exactly where we were. Sure enough, after waggling his thumbs he brought up an aerial view of the parking lot in which we were standing. Another thumb roll and the image became a street map, showing how we could walk from where we were standing to some other place.

"Get this," he said, as he waggled his way to a list of nearby pizza places.

A venture capital firm in Silicon Valley, Kleiner Perkins Caufield & Byers, put together a $200 million kitty for would-be apps inventors like me. So I figured the best way to cash in was to invent an app that computes the market for apps.

Turns out there are already several of those, including a site called 148apps.biz, which reported in 2013 that Apple's App Store had 807,014 active apps available for downloading. There were 216,016 people and businesses "publishing" these apps—with roughly 330 new apps submitted to Apple every day.

About a quarter of Apple's apps are free; about a third cost 99 cents, and a third cost more—with a few selling for over $450. One, called QSFF Stats, is designed for amateur players of flag football to track their performance. The price: $999.99.

Apple was in the app business for less than a year when it reached the one billion download mark, and by early 2013 the total exceeded 40 billion.

The app known as BubbleWrap allows users to press images of bubble wrap and hear a digitally-created popping sound, which to many consumers is a real gas. Speaking of which, when it comes to app sounds fart noises are among the most popular, starting with the renowned iFart. This app allows users to "Select randomly from 18 digitally mastered fart sounds for the ultimate in poop gas." An app called Bowel Mover allows you to track your digestive process.

Another big seller is iSteam, called "genius" by a critic at *The New York Times*, who must have been fiddling with his iPhone while sitting through a four-hour performance at Carnegie Hall. The app creates virtual condensation on your screen that you can "wipe" with your finger. Over two million have been downloaded at 99 cents.

A favorite free app is The Shut Up Button. You press it and your iPhone shouts "shut up." Another is called Have2P, which directs the user to the nearest public toilet and provides details about what each facility offers.

For reasons that escape me, Hold On! is a popular app with which you press an on-screen button while a timer keeps track of how long you can keep your finger on the button.

Full disclosure: I don't have the faintest idea how to go about inventing an app. My plan for this column was to acknowledge the phenomenal app market (all cited here are real), then come up with my own humorous concepts for fake apps. That was before I read about a real app called The AcneApp, which uses blue and red lights to supposedly kill skin bacteria. This scientifically unproven app is sold to iPhone users for $1.99. And the Hello Cow app, which sells for one dollar, and when you touch it you hear a mooing sound. That's it.

I planned to end my app spoof by declaring that I was marketing an app that doesn't do anything. Then I learned that a fellow named Paul Perry actually sells a 99-cent app called Nothing. Its ad says, "Nothing is everything you ever wanted in an application—except much, much less."

◆◆◆

Can the Internet Save Main Street?

If Tom Hanks and Meg Ryan ever decide to make a sequel to their 1998 charmer "You've Got Mail," the story line might go like this:

Happily married and still living in Manhattan, the couple has dropped AOL and now communicates exclusively by text, tweet and Skype. But as the film begins, the Fox & Sons mega-bookstore chain is in trouble. Kathleen Kelly-Fox, now executive vice president, tweets: "Sales down 63%. Internet taking best customers. E-books killing us."

Joe Fox, meanwhile, has given up quoting "The Godfather" and now speaks almost exclusively in lines from "Avatar." Standing in the deserted lobby of his giant store, he quips, "Everything is backwards now, like out there is the true world, and in here is the dream." A few days later, Fox & Sons files Chapter 11 and is shuttered.

But in the end the Foxes sell Joe's yacht and use the money to re-open The Shop Around the Corner, which now has a coffee bar and free Wi-Fi. Profits are modest, but the couple lives happily ever after because sales, while too small to sustain the big-box store, are just right for the needs of a hard-working, book-loving, Internet-addicted couple.

And the moral of the story is one few would have guessed: The Internet might save Main Street.

OK, maybe "save" is overstating it. But there is evidence that in some categories—books, and perhaps also video, electronics and toys—when giant chain stores go under, the door is reopened for the very locally operated independents they knocked out a decade or two ago.

The book business provides a particularly vivid example, because the big players like Barnes & Noble are being clobbered by Internet sales, via companies such as Amazon, as well as by online delivery of e-books. But few observers—even the most aggressive supporters of the digital frontier—are prepared to write off the segment of book buyers who will, for the foreseeable future, prefer to purchase books printed on paper in a retail setting that is more likely located on Main Street than at the mall.

New York Magazine reported on the success of 13 small, independent bookstores, noting that five of them had opened as a result of "the local-is-better ethos, which has bled over from the culinary and fashion worlds."

And there's plenty of supporting anecdotal evidence in other fields as well. For example, the closing of Circuit City's stores has led to the rebirth of local, hands-on electronics shops. The bankruptcy of K.B. Toys has allowed some local toy merchants to sneak back in. The fast-fading fortunes of Hollywood Video and Blockbuster have been blessings for neighborhood video stores like the one owned by Tom Tavares in Fall River, Mass. "We just concentrate on making people happy," he told the *Herald News* newspaper. "We're not looking to get rich."

That's probably a healthy perspective, because as video and books go increasingly digital and more shoppers go online, the crumbs left behind are not much to build on and won't last forever. But it's fascinating to watch the pendulum swing.

In the music industry, for instance, where digital sales account for about 37% of the U.S. business, sales of LPs and vinyl albums continue to grow—with much of the traffic in small, neighborhood shops.

So, if you're thinking of opening a store on Main Street, what's your best bet? The fastest growing online categories include: consumer electronics; sports and fitness; jewelry and watches; computers; home and garden; music and movies. It's a good bet that those are fields in which superstores will founder, allowing mom and pop to get back in business.

In the movie sequel, as the credits roll, Kathleen might text Joe: "Sold two books this morning to a sweet older gentleman from the Upper West Side. Said he's never seen a Kindle and hopes he never does. I think he'll be a regular customer :)"

THE MAIN STREET JOURNAL.

MONDAY, APRIL 1, 2013 · VOL. CCLIV NO. 85   **$.05

What's News -

New polls show that Barack Obama has his highest popularity with Americans who actually live on a street called Main Street. Data from Gallup show Obama with 96% approval among Main Street residents. A3

■ Republicans have increased popularity with voters who still reside on Wall Street in New York. The 14 registered voters are said to favor the GOP overwhelmingly.

■ Sales of librarian glasses have soared following Sarah Palin's latest appearances. A firm in Wasilla that markets the glasses worldwide says it can't keep up with the demand. A2

■ Congress will consider a measure to rename all U.S. streets Main Street. Backed by the GOP, "No Street Left Behind" will likely pass the House by voice vote. A4

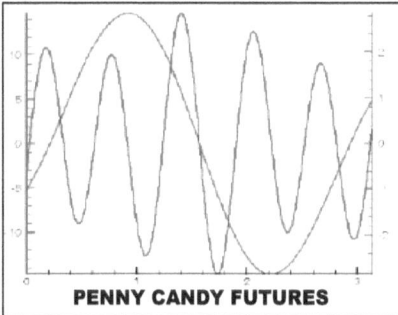

PENNY CANDY FUTURES

Obama Backs Bowling Bailout; McCain Seeks Six-Pack Subsidy

Seeking to ride the wave of enthusiasm for all things Main Street, both John McCain and Barack Obama have taken steps to bolster their appeal to voters who live on Main Street, or wish they did.

Obama said he will ask Congress to pass the bowling bailout bill without further delay. The Main Street measure would provide free insurance coverage to bowling establishments that have been hit by lawsuits over germs in older bowling shoes.

McCain, meanwhile told supporters in Mayberry, N.C., that government must step in to help. He told the crowd at the Main Street Tavern, "that we can't overlook the needs of Main Street during these difficult times. If Main Street wants a beer or two, then who are the bloodsucking CEOs on Wall Street to deny them?"

Democrats in Omaha, Neb., said they will move all campaign offices to addresses on Main Street. GOP aides said they were focusing efforts for 2014 on the "Battleground Streets" -- Main Street in Carson City, Nev., West Main Street, in Colebrook, N.H., and South Main Street in Dublin, Ohio.

WEATHER

Gray skies are going to clear up! Sunny days are on the way! Temperatures will be pleasant! Is the long-range outlook good? You betcha!

Journal Moves Headquarters To Des Moines, Cuts Newsstand Price to 5 Cents

By MAIN STREET STAFF

In a stunning acknowledgment of the depths to which Wall Street has sunk in the hearts and minds of Americans, News Corp. announced today that it will move all operations to Des Moines, Iowa. The company's flagship newspaper has been renamed The Main Street Journal.

"There's little left for us here," stated Rupert Murdoch as he packed for the trip to the Midwest. "No matter how much is spent to bailout Wall Street, it's clear that Main Street holds the future, not just for America but for the global economy."

Also today, The Journal slashed its cover price to 5 cents. Editors expected the new format to total six pages most days.

"The good news for us is that there are so few companies to cover, we can do it in much less space," explained the paper's editor in chief.

"Ironically, we have one column called Main Street. We'll add more."

YOUR GUIDE TO THE ALL NEW JOURNAL

♦**Peanuts, Blondie Join Our Comic Lineup!**

♦**Outdoor Column Covers Moose Hunt!**

♦**Market Graphics Now Feature Smiley Faces!**

Somewhere along the line, politicians became fascinated by Main Street, as if it were a single place. That prompted this bit of op-art that I put together for The Boston Globe.

www.caglecartoons.com

Google Is Watching

"There was of course no way of knowing whether you were being watched at any given moment ... It was even conceivable that they watched everybody all the time."

That quote from George Orwell's "1984" becomes increasingly prescient in light of developments in eavesdropping, pioneered by Google. The company now has a service called Latitude, which allows consenting users to monitor each other's whereabouts. It's the company's latest snooping tool, the most controversial being the Street Views photographic mapping service.

When I tried Street Views by entering my address, I was surprised to see that with a single click a truly Orwellian image popped onto the screen: my house, my car, the newspaper in the driveway. I could zoom in for a clear view of the open window on the second floor and the handy drainpipe that potential burglars might use to reach that window when no one was home.

Google has been working on Street Views since 2007, an incredibly tedious process. As remarkable as the computer results are, they still require hired motorists, known as GeoImmersive Data Producers, to drive up and down every street using 11 roof-mounted cameras to snap 360-degree images.

Boston was among the first cities captured by Street Views, and now Google has photographed every nook of the Bay State, both from ground level and from the perspective of satellites high in orbit.

When Street Views comes to a community, it often sparks great curiosity and raging debate about the propriety of Google's remarkable feat. To some it is an outrageous invasion of privacy—a true step toward the world Orwell envisioned. To others, including Google management, it is simply the latest beneficial—and commercially valuable —use of modern technology.

After first arguing that Street Views showed nothing more than could be seen by anyone traveling on public property, Google agreed to blur all identifiable faces and license plates. But by conceding that much, Google opens the door to demands that, say, doors should be blurred, and for that matter upstairs windows and drainpipes.

Of course it would be naive to think that Big Brother hasn't been watching for some time. From the all-too-obvious ceiling cameras in convenience stores to the government's exotic keyhole satellites, we're all photographed more often than we might care to believe.

When US Airways Flight 1549 went down unexpectedly in the Hudson River—not a likely spot for routine surveillance—hidden cameras on shore were able to capture it from several angles.

The federal government has already warned Google not to photograph military installations. Then there's North Oaks, Minnesota, whose city council contacted Google on behalf of its 4,500 residents, demanding that all photos taken within its borders be deleted.

Existing law makes distinctions between public property and private property; between public figures and private individuals. Yet in the Google Universe, these boundaries become fuzzy.

What if I created a reality show for which I stationed a TV crew on the public street outside your house, and spent weeks photographing your every move? What if I edited the footage to make the funniest three minutes—including the time you backed the car over the tulips, and the time you chased the neighbor's cat and slipped? And what if, unlike "Candid Camera," the program invented by my father Allen Funt, I televised it without your permission?

Or, what if I paid a team of Data Producers to go through thousands of Street Views, including the one with your home, looking for driveways in need of repair, then sold the list to a paving company?

With each technological breakthrough, some laws will require re-examination. So, too, will our definition of privacy.

As someone who, like my father, devoted many years to photographing unsuspecting people, I can report that the latest developments give me pause. It's one thing to have a brief, once-in-a-lifetime encounter with a hidden camera. It's another thing to live, as Orwell put it, "in the assumption that every sound you made was overheard, and, except in darkness, every movement scrutinized."

◆◆◆

Theater for Twits

Ladies and gentlemen, during this evening's performance, flash photography and video recording are strictly prohibited. Now, turn on your cellphones and enjoy the show!

In an unsavory confluence of social media and the arts, we now have what are known as the tweet seats—sections of otherwise dignified theaters where communicating via Twitter during shows is actually encouraged.

The Cincinnati Symphony Orchestra has tweet seats from which patrons can carry on what organizers call "digital conversations" during concerts. In Florida, the Palm Beach Opera set up a tweet section for a performance of "Madama Butterfly." To the surprise of many, The Public Theater in New York said via Twitter: "We think we may be the first of the large theaters to do some Tweet Seats, don't know about smaller theaters."

So what's the deal with tweeting and texting in theaters? Are promoters so desperate to attract younger audiences that they're willing to risk disrupting the experience for the majority of paying theatergoers? The answer, in five characters, is "u bet." Here's a suggestion for the Palm Beach Opera: Since you already have supertitles to provide the English translation, why not also display messages from the tweet seats? They could scroll along during the show, the way CNN and Fox News Channel often run distracting viewer tweets across the bottom of the TV screen during presidential debates.

There's plenty to learn via the thumbs of socially aware theater-goers. For example, according to actual postings during a concert featuring works of Mozart, furnished by the Cincinnati Symphony, withak53 wrote: "Music hall looks a lot prettier from the top balcony." And hippielunatic tweeted: "star spangled banner always chokes me up a bit in music hall."

It was in the film "Planes, Trains and Automobiles" that Steve Martin said to John Candy, "You know, everything isn't an anecdote." He advised, "Have a point. It makes it so much more interesting for the listener."

But Mr. Martin's quip was so 1987. Having a point doesn't seem to be important in today's text-as-you-view entertainment scene. It's all about the experience and the moment. At sporting events—where, mercifully, fans are not so easily bothered by the behavior of others in the crowd—texting while rooting has become practically mandatory. Sportswriters routinely tweet from the press box during games for the benefit of followers unable to wait for the post-game blog.

Several players have been discovered tweeting during games, among them Chad Ochocinco, who was once fined $25,000 by the N.F.L. for sending messages during a Cincinnati Bengals game. What's next? Plácido Domingo tweeting from backstage at The Met that the conductor failed to keep up with him during "The Enchanted Island"?

A cable-TV series coined a term for this before the advent of smartphones: "Short Attention Span Theater."

And once the tweeters become bored with Puccini, aren't they likely to fire up Words With Friends? How many in the "Madama Butterfly" audience are really playing Angry Birds? Perhaps the real goal of frightened theater managers is not so much to enhance the experience for the majority, for whom Mozart works just fine without tweets from the balcony, but to make the time go faster for those who barely tolerate the arts but may have purchased a ticket as, say, a favor to their companion.

Or maybe it's just for members of the Twitter-tethered community who believe Mozart is best enjoyed in 140 notes.

◆◆◆

Link to This

There are several things, Barack Obama, that I'm going to do, Tea Party and guns, to promote what I write, Lady Gaga, and generate more buzz, oil-covered birds.

The first is to include lots of "tags," like those above, in the first sentence so that Internet searchers are directed to my articles whether they care about them or not. It's part of my SEO, or search engine optimization.

A message from Bud: This column's for you.

The preceding sentence is an example of advertising that I'll be placing within my reports. I'll also be selling product-placement plugs, but unlike my ads, which will be identified, the plugs will be designed to fool readers who won't realize that when I mention driving to the scene of a story in, say, an all-new 2013 Odyssey with its aggressive stance and sporty lightning bolt beltline, that I'm actually getting paid by Honda.

I'm going to launch a blog in which I'll ramble about the exciting things that happen to me while writing columns. I'll blog about how my mother always phones to see if I've written anything funny, and how we spend the next hour trying to come up with an entry for *The New Yorker* magazine's weekly cartoon caption contest, which we never win, even though I seriously believe many of my entries have been superior to those the judges picked. And who, exactly, are these judges anyway?

I'll also be able to blog about a lot of stuff that editors and readers keep telling me no one cares about, but which I think are kind of interesting. For instance, I intend to blog about how UPS drivers used to drive while standing up, but then they were told they were required to wear seatbelts so they had to sit down. I've got hundreds of words of blogable thoughts on things like that.

I'm installing a webcam on my computer so readers will be able to go online and watch me write 24/7. In order to make it more compelling, and to address the fact that I only manage to write 2/5, I've placed a monitor behind my desk so lurkers can see LolCats.com in the background.

From now on I'm going to tweet when I get an idea for a story. For example: "researching Joe Biden fave BBQ recipes."

I've hired hourly workers in Singapore to develop apps for my columns. So far they've come up with an app that tells what time it is wherever I'm writing.

On the advice of industry pundits, I've decided not to erect a pay wall around my content. This is a huge gamble, because with millions and millions of Net surfers out there, if just one would pay me $19.95 per month, I'd have almost $20.

This is kind of cool: I'm going to record myself reading everything I write and make it available as a podcast. I've often heard that audiences enjoy letting their imaginations run wild when listening to writers painting delightful word pictures, so I'll be offering my downloads for just 99 cents.

From now on, you'll find a considerable number of hyperlinks in my writing. These can be annoying, I know, because they're going to appear in different colors and some will be underlined. On the bright side, I'll be sending readers to sites that will pay me money for each click.

I'm going to offer RSS feeds as soon as I learn more about how to do that.

I think this new "model" is going to provide me with more lift than I've been getting with the old model, which I first developed when they stopped selling ribbons for my IBM Selectric.

I'm sure to wind up with many new followers, Justin Bieber.

STILL THE GREAT PASTIME

Baseball's Booze Problem

For several seasons, fans may recall, many baseball telecasts began with announcers reading the commercial line: "Grab an ice cold Bud." Beginning in 2012, the pitch changed to: "Grab some Buds."

Whether the purpose of the new blurb is to cleverly link friends—"buds"—with consuming multiple beers—"Buds"—during games is something only the folks at Anheuser-Busch and its ad agency know for sure. What is certain is that baseball, along with other pro sports, has a drinking problem.

Beer has long been baseball's beverage of choice. As a kid I listened to Yankee games and sang along with the jingle: "Baseball and Ballantine...what a combination, all across the nation..." The announcer, Mel Allen, referred to home runs as "Ballantine Blasts."

With due respect to apple pie, nothing is more American than watching a baseball game with a hot dog and a beer. But lately things have gotten out hand.

The problem's epicenter since 2011 is Dodger Stadium in Los Angeles, where on Opening Day in April two unidentified Dodger supporters attacked a fan of the visiting Giants, Bryan Stow, leaving him sprawled in the parking lot with critical injuries. Snow wasn't even able to speak until September. While it's not clear what role alcohol may have played, the Dodgers saw a direct link and immediately revised the stadium's alcohol policies.

For years the Dodgers were baseball's most cavalier franchise when it came to pushing alcohol sales and tolerating the rowdy behavior that resulted. Patrons were allowed to purchase two 24-ounce beers at a time—the equivalent of four "normal" beers—and the Dodgers began selling hard liquor as well. Following the Stow incident, the Dodgers cancelled plans for their half-price beer days.

Rules regarding alcohol sales vary widely among the 30 Major League teams and at the hundreds of minor league venues. Some stadiums, such as AT&T Park in San Francisco, do not permit beer sales by vendors in the stands. At other locations, such as Miller Park in Milwaukee—named after a beer company—vendors do hawk beer.

Many minor league teams, such as the Fresno Grizzlies in California, have special "one dollar beer nights." At a stadium I visited in New Jersey they call it Thirsty Thursday—an invitation to over-indulge. In 2013, the California League (Class A) began selling Baseball Beer, said by its maker to be designed to drink while watching games.

Research published by the University of Minnesota indicates that roughly 40 percent of fans leaving pro baseball and football games have measurable alcohol levels in their systems, and 8 percent of fans are legally drunk. The proportion of drunken fans rises dramatically among two groups: those under age 35, and those who have tailgated before the game.

At Fenway Park, an increase in beer sales led to complaints about intoxicated fans. Still, the Red Sox obtained permission to sell hard liquor, but only after agreeing to keep it away from the bleachers. Many teams seem to believe that the best way to deal with alcohol abuse is to sell mixed drinks only in the "luxury" boxes and "premium" seats.

This approach is part of a larger trend to aggressively segregate fans according to economic considerations. True, box seats have always cost more than the bleachers. But at newer parks the higher-priced sections are built in such a way that fans with less expensive tickets can't so much as set foot there, meaning they can't access the elite concession stands.

Such policies may make wealthy fans feel safer, but they often lead to unrestricted rowdiness in the cheap seats, which, at Dodger Stadium, were overtaken by beer-guzzling thugs.

Baseball's drinking problem extends to the players as well, with an alarming number of Major Leaguers arrested for drunk driving. The issue of drinking by ballplayers has been of concern since the 2007 death of St. Louis Cardinals pitcher Josh Hancock, who was legally drunk when he crashed his car following a game.

Major League baseball, still attempting to recover from the scandal involving performance-enhancing drugs, has struggled to craft an alcohol policy for players. But Commissioner Bud Selig must also create an over-arching alcohol policy for fans.

Tailgating should be eliminated, as should beer sales by roving vendors. No alcohol should be sold after six innings, and reduced-price beer banned entirely. Hard liquor policies need reevaluation.

Rather than leaving alcohol controls to individual owners, Major League baseball should acknowledge its responsibility to act before there are other serious incidents. In other words, Commissioner Selig, this Bud's for you.

◆◆◆

Spit Ball

Sights and sounds of a glorious new baseball season arrive each spring: the emerald green grass, the crack of the bat, the endless globs of spit.

If owners really want to clean up the Great American Pastime, they should start by doing something about the spitting epidemic. Spits per inning is the only Major League stat that seems to rise unfailingly each season.

It's reached the point where any television close-up of a ballplayer lasting more than three seconds is sure to include at least one spit shot. I suppose viewers watching in HD on wide screens should be grateful that TV directors don't replay this action in super slo-mo.

How it began is no mystery: many ballplayers chewed tobacco, as some still do, and had little choice but to spit the stuff all over the diamond. Tobacco products have been banned in the Minor Leagues since 1993, but that hasn't reduced spitting one bit.

Funny thing, while pro football and basketball players have their share of gross habits, you rarely see them spitting. Perhaps indoor courts cause NBA players to think twice about expectorating; maybe helmets make it too difficult for NFL players to spit on the field. Pro golfers and tennis players hardly ever spit—at least not on national TV —so what's with baseball players?

Spitting is so integral to baseball that it used to be part of the skill set. The spitball was a legal pitch prior to 1920, and when it was finally banned, pitchers throwing the spitter were allowed to continue until they retired. The last legal spitballer in the Majors is believed to have been Burleigh Grimes of the Dodgers, who tossed his germ-laden pitch well into the 1930s.

In the modern era, Tim Lincecum of the Giants is one of the game's brightest stars, and also one of its most frequent spitters. It's no exaggeration to say that when TV cameras focus on Lincecum in the dugout he spits every three-to-five seconds. Considering that games take roughly three hours, and he pitches once every five games, Lincecum spits in the dugout about 315,360 times per season.

Back in 2004, management of the Yankees was sufficiently irked about spitting that they allowed me to do a "Candid Camera" gag in which I posed as an exec from the commissioner's office, informing players that spitting had gotten out of hand. Nick Johnson sheepishly explained that during games his mouth just, you know, fills up and he's got no choice but to spit. Jorge Posada seemed genuinely concerned when I told him the commissioner's office had charted the Yankee catcher spitting several thousand times the previous season.

I came away realizing that: (a) most Major Leaguers are very nice fellows, (b) they don't realize how frequently they spit during games, and (c) they'll never stop, whether management likes it or not.

Yet, in Minnesota the Twins were confronted by a petition from fans, demanding that beautiful Target Field remain relatively spit-free. "Whereas the habit of spitting is acknowledged to be, along with careless coughing and sneezing, a hazard to good health," the petition said, "and whereas TV cameras filming Twins games picture dugouts in which spitting is regularly observed; and whereas children are known to admire and imitate managers, coaches and professional athletes such as the Minnesota Twins in their actions both in the dugout and on the playing field..." and, after several more whereases: please stop spitting.

There's no evidence that players on the Twins or any other teams are expectorating less than before.

Maybe that's just as well. If there's one good thing about the constant spitting in baseball, it's that it helps keep our minds off all the televised crotch grabbing.

◆◆◆

Baseball's Bat and Gall

As a lifelong baseball fan, I wish the game no ill. But you know what I hope? I hope that when someone is seriously injured by a broken bat, the victim gets a good lawyer and sues Major League Baseball for many millions of dollars, and wins.

Then, of course, the dangerous types of wooden bats—the ones that break in half and fly across the diamond and increasingly into the stands—will be banned. Why baseball is waiting for it to play out this way, as it surely will, is beyond batty.

At one point, MLB was sufficiently concerned about the danger of broken bats to commission a study. Three months of research led to some superficial "guidelines" for bat manufacturers and, of course, a plan to conduct additional studies.

Meanwhile, bats are breaking with alarming frequency. During one game, a shortstop for the Red Sox, Nick Green, found himself trying to field a ball and dodge a broken bat simultaneously. He opted to deflect the bat barrel with his arm as the ball went between his legs. The splintered bat head stuck in the ground like a lawn dart.

"Lord, that was very scary," said then-manager Manny Acta, whose Nationals team faced the Sox that day. "We have seen bats split in two in the last couple of years, but I've never seen a bat travel that far and that fast toward that guy."

A few days later, the Giants' Pablo Sandoval broke his bat, sending both the bat head and the ball beyond the second baseman. During his very next time up, Sandoval's replacement bat broke in a similar way, and this time the splintered bat head went flying into the stands behind first base. This is all too routine.

The problem is with maple bats, which, according to MLB's research, are three times more likely to break into separate pieces than bats made of ash. Maple bats have been used by Major League players for only about 15 years, but they soared in popularity after Barry Bonds turned to maple (and other substances) to set the record for homers in a single season in 2001. Since then, the ranks of players using maple bats has climbed to about 60 percent.

Many factors contribute to broken bats—from their size and shape to the condition of the wood from which they are made. But the major concern among ballplayers and fans is that maple bats, although roughly 20 percent harder than ash, tend to break into sharp, jagged pieces.

In Los Angeles, a bat barrel fractured the jaw of a woman seated behind the visitors' dugout at Dodger Stadium. In another incident, Don Long, a coach with the Pirates, was hit in the face with a flying piece of a maple bat as he sat in the dugout. And during a game between the Rockies and Royals, home plate umpire Brian O'Nora was hit on the head by a chunk of a maple bat.

Ironically, Bonds' record notwithstanding, there is no scientific evidence that hitters do better with maple bats. But players' habits are difficult to change, and a ban on maple would require collective bargaining between MLB and the players' union.

There are economic considerations as well, since as many as 30 companies are now licensed to make maple bats for the Big Leagues.

But it's not as if baseball hasn't ever been forced by tragic circumstances to implement new safety precautions. In 2007, a minor-league coach for the Tulsa Drillers was struck in the head by a line drive as he stood near first base. Mike Coolbaugh's legacy is that his death led to the rule that all base coaches must wear protective helmets.

Why must there be another Mike Coolbaugh before baseball does away with dangerous bats?

◆◆◆

BUSTS at the Ballpark

Baseball has a stat for everything: WHIP (walks and hits per innings pitched), LIPS (late inning pressure situations), ERA and IRA (earned runs allowed and inherited runs allowed), plus dozens more. But as my math teacher was fond of saying, "Garbage in means garbage out."

Baseball's nagging problem is what I call BUSTS (bad umpiring and scoring tarnishes stats).

Players and fans alike are losing patience with inconsistencies among Major League umpires and official scorers. What good is a pitcher's K/BB (strikeout-to-walk ratio) if umps can't agree on the strike zone? How important is a player's fielding percentage if scorers differ widely in determining what is a hit and what is an error?

The biggest beef with umps is that the strike zone, although clearly defined in the rules, is called differently by almost every official. It's so bad that Mike Krukow, the former pitcher and veteran color commentator in San Francisco, begins each telecast by explaining the whims of that day's home plate ump. Analyzing umpire Alan Porter, for example, Mr. Krukow said: "He can have a weird zone, it's a little inconsistent." In the same telecast, he added, "On getaway day, umpires are more likely to call a strike on a checked swing."

Many fans, myself included, appreciate the human element in baseball—even among umpires—and oppose suggestions that fancy electronic tools and more instant replays should be added to the game. But there is no reason why Major League Baseball can't insist upon a standard interpretation of the strike zone. If an ump blows a call, so be it, but no ump should be allowed to invent his own rules. Chipper Jones, the former Braves superstar, raised eyebrows one season when he candidly labeled umpiring "substandard."

Official scoring is even worse—so much so that MLB finally took steps to deal with the gross inconsistencies. Joe Torre, former Yankee and Dodger manager, took on the chore of reviewing controversial scoring decisions and, on occasion, ordering that an error be changed to a hit or vice versa.

Following a Yankees-A's game, for example, Mr. Torre decided the scorer was wrong to charge Oakland's Coco Crisp with an error on an outfield fly. The decision had a domino effect in the record books, with changes to the stats of the fielder, hitter and pitcher.

In most cases, scoring seems to protect fielders while boosting offensive stats. Too windy? Hit. Bad bounce? Hit. Ball falls while two fielders stare at each other? Hit. Sun in fielder's eyes (even if he had sunglasses resting on his hat but declined to wear them)? Hit.

During the 2012 All-Star game, outfielder Bryce Harper stood with a confused expression as Mike Napoli's routine fly dropped to the ground. Ruling: a hit. Come on.

How about the routine grounder that is bobbled by a fielder and results in a single out when a double play was possible? It's not an error because, as the infamous scoring axiom has it, "you can't assume a double play." Why the heck not?

The trend to favor fielders is unmistakable. The 11 highest fielding percentages of all time have come in the last 11 seasons, and overall errors are down by about 25 percent since 1970.

Scorers will sometimes check with a player after the game to get his opinion about a ruling. Sounds charitable, but that's not how officiating is supposed to work.

MLB insists its goal is to remove as much subjectivity as possible from both scoring and umpiring. But Mr. Torre shouldn't have to be changing scoring decisions after watching replays on his office TV, and players shouldn't require a pregame tutorial on how the home plate umpire will interpret balls and strikes.

As the season heats up, most of us watching from the bleachers or the couch are rooting for fewer ifs, ands...and BUSTS.

◆ ◆ ◆

Free Agent Fans

TEMPE, Ariz.—Under the brilliant desert sun that helps make spring training baseball a time of awakening for players and fans, the game's best hitter is blasting away in the batting cage. He looks as sharp as ever, so why should I care that Albert Pujols' red jersey now says Angels rather than Cardinals?

I'm finished being a sucker. Like many liberated fans, I no longer care about teams as much as individual players.

This is part of a gradual, but unmistakable shift that began decades ago when free agency set players loose and sports franchises started moving from one city to another. Until recently, however, fans were stuck with the local team and its roster.

Now, if you're a Pujols fan in St. Louis, where he hit 445 homers and batted .328 for 11 glorious years, you can root for him just as easily with his L.A. team. You can see every game he plays on satellite TV or computer and read details of his performance on Internet blogs. You can still have him on your fantasy baseball team. And you can frequent his website (Pujolsfive.com), like him on Facebook, or follow his tweets (@PujolsFive).

Many fans are still inclined to think of the local team as being "us," in a civic-minded sort of way, overlooking the fact that pro athletes and their employers are in the entertainment business. Nothing wrong with that. But the notion that fans should slavishly root for a particular team no matter whom it hires or where it opts to play is passé.

One of the best examples involved Jeremy Lin, the 23-year-old Harvard grad who leaped from obscurity to become one of the NBA's hottest players. Like many fans, I immediately started watching his games with the New York Knicks on satellite, although where he happened to play was irrelevant. I lost interest, but his fans had no trouble following Lin to the Houston Rockets.

By placing most games on satellite and computer, teams have encouraged fans to find freedom. And media support it with highlights that increasingly emphasize individual achievements—from "Web Gems" to the "Dunks of the Day."

It's quite different, of course, at the amateur level, where Little League and scholastic sports appropriately inspire community allegiance, while teaching kids about teamwork and loyalty. With pro sports, however, there are few teams I'd care to root for any more than I root for, say, FedEx or Starbucks—to name businesses I admire but whose logos I'd never wear on a shirt or hat unless they paid me to do it.

To be sure, some sports franchises are more worthy of respect than others. The Green Bay Packers, for example, are owned by roughly 112,000 of their fans. The Angels and their owner Arte Moreno, who lured Pujols, operate possibly the most fan-friendly organization in pro sports. But generally, there is no real fun in rooting for corporations unless you're a shareholder.

Sports have always provided the great American metaphors, so you have to wonder if our attitude toward athletes reflects a wider societal trend. After all, manufacturers, just like sports franchises, don't give a hoot about leaving town if they can find a better deal. We hire a million or so soldiers to handle our wars, and then fail to cheer them on like we once did. Our politicians behave increasingly like free agent athletes, looking out for themselves and seeking the biggest endorsement deals when they retire.

Fortunately, sports offers simpler choices. I still root for one team over another during specific games, and I continue to give an extra measure of emotional support to the teams from the region where I live. But that's it. I refuse to be part of, say, the Red Sox Nation as if it deserved the same allegiance as an actual country, and if the score disappoints me, I won't bleed Dodger Blue.

Here at spring training in Arizona I'm rooting for a dozen players on a half-dozen different teams. I find that free agency works as well in the stands as it does on the field.

◆◆◆

Minor League Monikers

After nearly 50 years without a pro team, baseball fans in Allentown, Pa., celebrated in 2008 with the arrival of a local club to cheer for. And the cheer is: "Go, Pigs!"

Actually, the team's official name is the Lehigh Valley IronPigs, Triple-A affiliate of the Philadelphia Phillies. But fans were quick to shorten the name, and a local reporter wasted no time titling his Internet column "The Hog Blog."

It's part of the charm of minor league baseball, which many fans have come to love as an alternative to Big League drug scandals, Big League egos, and, of course, $7.50 Big League beer. Most minor league baseball—even in Colorado Springs, Colo., where the Sky Sox play at 6,531 feet—is very much down to earth.

It's immediately evident in team names. The Major Leagues have always been content to name teams after mundane things such as cute little birds (Cardinals, Orioles, Blue Jays) or items of clothing (White Sox, Red Sox). Troubled by this, owners of the Tampa Devil Rays decided it was time for a fresh approach, so after considerable market research the team unveiled its dynamic new name in 2008: the Rays. Presumably the second-place choice was the Devils.

That's why you've gotta love the IronPigs, said by *Forbes* to be the nation's second most valuable minor-league franchise. Or the squad in Davenport, Iowa, which calls itself the Quad Cities River Bandits. Or the team in Casper, Wyo., renamed the Casper Ghosts.

For decades, minor league teams were stuck with the boring names of their Major League parent clubs. There remains a lot of that, with teams such as the Pawtucket Red Sox, Tampa Yankees, and Iowa Cubs each still saddled with the Big League moniker. But imagine the excitement rooting for the Albuquerque Isotopes (a name based on an episode of "The Simpsons"); the Brooklyn Cyclones (honoring the famous ride at Coney Island); the Augusta Greenjackets (the prize given winners of the Masters golf tournament), or the Vermont Lake Monsters (proudly perpetuating rumors of a beast in Lake Champlain).

In Savannah, Georgia, they've got the Sand Gnats. In Lansing, Michigan, the team goes by the name Lugnuts. And in Batavia, New York, the loveable locals are known as the Muckdogs.

In Idaho Falls, the team used to be named after a potato and was known as the Russets, but now it's named after a partridge and is called the Idaho Falls Chukars. There are actually a lot of bird names in the minor leagues, they just tend to be more exotic than their Big League counterparts. How about the Great Lakes (Michigan) Loons, the Delmarva, Md., Shorebirds, and perhaps the most famous team in minor league history, the Toledo Mud Hens. Toledo's Triple-A team has borne the long-legged marsh bird's name since 1896.

Some minor league organizations conduct team-naming contests. A few years back there were over 2,800 suggestions for what to call a team in Alabama, resulting in: the Montgomery Biscuits. Between innings hot biscuits are fired into the crowd.

Fans in Reno, Nevada, were asked to suggest a name for the Triple-A team that began play there in 2009. The Reno Roulette? That's got nice alliteration, but organized baseball has never felt comfortable acknowledging organized gambling. Since Nevada has no corporate income tax, how about the Reno Refunds? As a city that stays up late, the Reno Revelers? Or, considering the large population of retirees, the Reno Wrinkles? Reno's fans finally settled on the Aces.

Few teams can compete with the pure simplicity of the name worn by the Class-A club in Modesto, Calif., where almond trees cover the landscape. When a bad play is made on the diamond, fans simply call out the team's name, "Nuts!"

Modern minor-league monikers reflect an ingredient that often seems lost among Major League franchises: fun. And when it comes to the Great American Pastime, that's really the name of the game.

◆◆◆

WE ARE WHAT WE WATCH

It's Not Democracy. It's a Sub.

What's your vote? Is America's newfangled fascination with being polled, minute by minute, on every imaginable topic, reflective of (a) a more informed population, (b) renewed responsibility among media or (c) none of the above?

Here's a vote for "c."

Despite a sorry track record when it comes to voter turnout in government elections, Americans have become positively wild about other types of voting. Hundreds of polls are conducted every day on topics ranging from how to wage the war in Afghanistan to which YouTube video is the day's best.

Isn't it remarkable that at the very time when so many of us are baffled by the mixed up state of things—from economy to environment, from unprincipled politicians to wayward celebrities—we have simultaneously become obsessed with tracking our feelings about everything? Perhaps it was inevitable that a society whose texts, tweets, posts and IMs seem to be volumizing in inverse proportion to the importance of the messages it sends, now demands instant status reports on what it is thinking.

NBC's "Today" show once devoted an entire week to electing "America's Best Sandwich." The candidates, each of which received plenty of free airtime, were: the muffuletta, from New Orleans; Katz's pastrami, from New York's landmark deli; the Philly cheesesteak; Sam's lobster roll, from Central California; and Frenchy's triple-decker, from Chicago. Remarkably, after watching close-ups of the "Today" hosts wolfing down these sandwiches for five straight days, tens of thousands of Americans felt qualified to vote without ever having tasted a morsel themselves. They elected the cheesesteak.

A CNN poll, conducted with Opinion Research Corporation, revealed that 74 percent of Americans believe George Washington told lies during his presidency—although pollsters never asked how on earth respondents came to that conclusion. MSNBC conducts its share of ludicrous online polls such as, "Which is your favorite Sesame Street Muppet?"

To some extent the deluge of daily voting is merely an inexpensive use of technology to fill overabundant media time. It is apparent that a segment of the public enjoys having its opinions collected and then re-gurgitated as a form of rapid, if unscientific, "news."

Yet America's fascination with voting does not seem to translate into increased participation in government elections.

Turnout in presidential elections has held steady at roughly 50 percent of the voting-age population for the past 75 years. The United States placed 120th among 169 nations for which data exists on voter turnout, falling between the Dominican Republic and Benin, according to a 2012 study by the Institute for Democracy and Electoral Assis-tance. Australia ranked highest, with voter turnout exceeding 94 per-cent.

Modern scientific polling has been around since George Gallup founded the American Institute of Public Opinion in 1936; soon there-after FDR became the first U.S. president to use polling to shape policy. In decades that followed, opinion tracking became omnipresent in sales, marketing, education, entertainment—indeed, in almost every facet of our lives. The explosion of instant digital communications in the '90s resulted in a geometric increase in surveying and data collec-tion.

But beyond ease of execution, what really drives this seemingly insatiable thirst for social summarizing? Is it that we know so much and care so deeply that we feel the need to weigh our opinions against the rest of the populace? Or are we largely ill-informed and less confi-dent—to the point of seeking to form our views through constant im-mersion in the opinions of others?

A small yet illustrative example of the trend in collective thinking is the practice by many news organizations of charting which online stories are most read and most e-mailed. A story that is popular thus becomes even more popular simply because of its popularity.

Daniel Yankelovich, a dean among pollsters, once said on PBS that he would be skeptical of any poll on a topic about which most people have not made up their minds. Ask yourself, he advised, if you have made up your own mind. If not, regard the polling data with caution.

The most robust example of a nation eager to be counted is provided by the television series "American Idol," which each season registers over half a billion votes (multiple votes allowed) by phone and text message to elect a winning performer. In contrast, about 129 million votes were cast in the 2012 presidential election. It's clear why marketers and politicians are examining new polling options.

By 2016 or 2020 there could be a serious movement to have voting in presidential elections conducted via the Internet. This will raise questions about the nature of democracy. On the one hand, Americans have a constitutional right to vote, and the specter of citizens standing for hours in the rain or being harassed at the polls understandably prompts efforts to find more user-friendly voting methods. On the other hand, the electoral process benefits from some degree of effort by voters—whether that involves taking time to study the issues or hiking to a polling place.

So, is the torrent of polling in America (a) evidence of a more involved citizenry, (b) a glimpse at the future of U.S. politics or (c) proof that Americans, with enough mouse clicks, might someday put a cheesesteak sandwich in the White House?

Our Daily Content

Perhaps by now you've formed an opinion about my writing. Well, you can call my work anything you like, as long as you don't call it "content."

For those who take their creativity seriously, content has become a dirty word.

With so much space to fill on the Internet and the cable dial, not to mention satisfying the seemingly endless needs of iThis and iThat, it's all about content. I've sat through lengthy industry dissertations about how media can't get enough video content, audio content and, of course, written content—but the term itself blurs the line between good content and bad content.

Imagine going to a restaurant hoping to get a culinary treat and instead learning you'll be served a plate of "kitchen content." How about if you went to pick up your suit at the cleaners and were handed a bag of "laundry content."

If this were only a semantic shortcut it would be no big deal. But lumping together the efforts of writers, musicians, videographers and so many other hard working creative folks and calling it content is not only demeaning, it's also part of the mindset that devalues creativity—by underpaying, plagiarizing and repackaging it to the disadvantage of reputable creators.

Much of what's published on the Internet these days comes from companies known as "content farms." It's difficult to imagine a more abhorrent term for what passes as journalism, but it's a billion-dollar business at places like Demand Media, a leading farm that harvests roughly 4,000 "pieces of content" each day.

On its own sites, such as eHow.com and Golflink.com, as well as for outside clients ranging from the newspaper *USA Today* to the fashion guru Tyra Banks, Demand develops its content by monitoring words and topics sought in Internet searches, then paying freelancers to create short articles and videos to address the supposed need.

One eHow contributor named "Jenajera" describes herself as a mother of four living in the Pacific Northwest and a "paralegal-turned-SEO-writer." (SEO is a slick term meaning "search engine optimization.") She has written such reports as "How to Determine the Value of Scrap Gold" and "How to Choose a Site for a Backyard Chicken Coop." But perhaps her most enlightening piece is "How to Make Money Writing eHow Articles," in which she notes that her most recent story "has earned me nearly $1 in less than a week"—from ad revenue that Demand Media shares with some writers on top of a fee of about $15.

Her advice: "The key to optimizing your earnings is to create a large cache of targeted, keyword heavy articles quickly." Also: "You will make more money from your eHow articles if you choose topics that are well supported by advertisers."

I have no beef with Jenajera or thousands of others like her, who undoubtedly work hard for each dollar Demand Media pays them. But, as the axiom has it, you get what you pay for, and it's fair to say readers of Demand's content aren't getting much.

Still, low-cost, low-quality content has a certain appeal. Media analyst Tish Grier, writing for the respected Poynter journalism site, goes so far as to suggest that companies like Demand Media could help struggling newspapers stay afloat by providing "edited, optimized evergreen content at reasonable cost."

That's true, I suppose, just as optimized toys can be purchased at reasonable cost from China.

It remains a possibility that as new media become more established, and the fascination wears off, things will change for the better. After all, the earliest material for television involved harvesting content from radio, until viewers demanded more. And when cable emerged as a programming force, ESPN, for example, cared so little about the quality of its fare that it devoted hours to rugby and Australian Rules Football, until fans grew tired of cheap sports content.

In the end, it's not all just "content," anymore than it's all just laundry, which is why the public must continue to demand the most from its media.

♦ ♦ ♦

Empty Interviews

Electronic news media have made enormous strides when it comes to speed, volume and diversity, but technology has not improved everything in the information marketplace.

There are more live interviews on television than ever before, but the quality is remarkably weak, due primarily to the personal agendas and sloppy efforts of interviewers. This is regrettable, because interviews remain a distinctive feature of electronic journalism and, when done well, provide information that significantly supplements our understanding of issues and individuals.

Consider an interview Lawrence O'Donnell conducted on MSNBC with the filmmaker and activist Michael Moore. Mr. Moore spoke a total of 1,034 words, while Mr. O'Donnell—whose job, after all, was to ask questions—spoke almost as many: 900.

The host was so intent on both asking and answering questions that at one point Mr. Moore said jokingly, "Thanks, Lawrence, for coming on the show tonight."

I happen to be among O'Donnell's fans, if for no other reason than he helped produce my favorite TV series, "The West Wing." Yet, like the interviews of many cable-TV hosts, O'Donnell's often seem designed to showcase his own views rather than to draw out interesting opinions from guests. Chris Matthews of MSNBC and Sean Hannity of Fox News Channel do the same irritating thing, making it hard for guests to get a word in edgewise.

During one interview with Mitt Romney, Mr. Hannity asked 10 questions, one of which was 172 words long and lasted 51 seconds, while two others went on for over 100 words. It was as if the host were filibustering his own guest.

Not long ago, television journalists preferred to pre-record interviews whenever possible—still the norm on magazine programs such as CBS's "60 Minutes"—while politicians and other newsmakers favored going live. That's because editing allows reporters to clean up and even re-record questions to their advantage, while making cuts that are sometimes to the guest's disadvantage. As Barbara Walters once told me when I interviewed her about interviewing, "Whoever holds the scissors ultimately controls the message."

Nowadays, cable news programs favor live interviews because they add immediacy and are a natural byproduct of improved technology. This gives politicians and other guests more power, while exposing interviewers' ineptitude.

Newsmakers have taken advantage of the live interview format to work in more talking points and even to scold hosts when the questions are tough. In an interview on CBS, Rick Santorum pounced on host Charlie Rose when Mr. Rose asked about statements by a major campaign donor regarding contraception. "This is the same gotcha politics that you get from the media," said Mr. Santorum, "and I'm not going to play that game."

A telling sign of a poorly conducted interview is when reporters ask questions and then supply possible answers, creating a multiple-choice quiz—which might work in a classroom but usually flops on TV. Sports interviewers have come to favor the non-question, in which the interviewee is simply asked to "talk," as in, "Talk about that winning shot."

Interview questions should come quickly and cleanly. Yet on a broadcast of CBS's "Face the Nation," Bob Schieffer began two questions of Newt Gingrich with the extraneous phrase, "Let me ask you," and then he asked consecutive questions of Ron Paul that began, "Let me ask you this question." On CNN's "State of the Union," Candy Crowley asked six questions during one program that all began with forms of "Let me ask . . ."

The best interviewers do their homework, put their own opinions aside, keep questions brief, and listen closely for possible follow-ups. Live interviews are among the few elements in journalism not significantly affected by technology; they can't be replaced by blogs or tweets. But TV hosts too often fall short.

Fox analyst Brit Hume, a frequent contributor on Bill O'Reilly's program, joked about what it's like being interviewed on cable TV. Noting that he had driven to Florida while listening to the audio version of Mr. O'Reilly's book, "Killing Lincoln," Mr. Hume quipped to Mr. O'Reilly that it was just like being on his show: "You talked and I listened."

◆◆◆

Stuck in the Spin Cycle

Rhetorical spinning used to be good sport. Think back on the scenes following Presidential debates, when high-powered advocates for each candidate pounced on reporters to spin every syllable so it seemed to favor their team's point of view. It was unabashedly biased, and usually entertaining.

Nowadays, though, we're stuck in a constant spin cycle, and it's enough to make most of us dizzy.

The Internet, cable-TV, talk radio, all provide forums for differing voices to publish and be heard. In theory, this broadened exposure to wide ranging perspectives makes us better informed and more receptive to opposing points of view. Yet, just the opposite is happening. In many respects, what's referred to as the digital information explosion has proved to be a time bomb.

Say you favor lower taxes for people driving red convertibles. Then you undoubtedly bookmark the Lower Taxes for People Driving Red Convertibles blog. There, every news report, every quote, every snippet of polling data is spun to reinforce your views. Those with opposing beliefs, folks who happen to support higher taxes for people driving red convertibles, are demonized and mocked. Of course, they're too busy to notice, since the spin is quite different on their fa-vorite site: Higher Taxes for People Driving Red Convertibles.

When it comes to hot-button topics like health care or taxes, if you watched Fox News Channel and MSNBC side by side, you'd have thought they were covering entirely different stories. One camp calls the other "socialists"; the other refers to its philosophical opponents as "wackos." Token appearances by weak-kneed guests, who dare spin in the opposite direction, rarely put dents in the dialogue.

It's even worse on radio. Advo-casters, some of whom host both radio and TV shows, tend to spin more recklessly when it's audio only. Radio rants are frequently more outrageous and blatantly biased, yet, despite vast audiences, go largely unheard by those with opposing views.

Rather than stretching our minds with new media, we spend an inordinate amount of time these days doing what is indelicately re-ferred to as drinking our own bath water.

Occasionally the process is thrown a curve—a pitch that is hard to hit precisely because of its spin. Such was the case when the Obama Administration announced a revamped policy to allow some explora-tion for offshore oil. Anti-Obama spinmeisters, who tend to favor off-shore drilling, deemed it too little too late, and probably some sort of socialist ploy. Pro-Obama spinsters proclaimed the move shrewd poli-tics aimed at winning conservative support for more important envi-ronmental issues.

The most popular news guy on cable-TV, Fox's Bill O'Reilly, de-cided early on to spin the entire spin situation to his advantage by la-beling his show a "No Spin Zone." That's quite clever because it ac-knowledges the spin problem without actually doing anything about it—much as Fox proclaims itself "Fair and Balanced," while striving for little of either.

When you freeze the frames on our media and our politics, it's dif-ficult to tell which is currently exerting the greatest spin on the other. Media have become more fractionalized and narrowly focused on sin-gular points of view. Politicians and their supporters have grown in-tolerant and less inclined to compromise.

Conventional media whose goals, at least in theory, are to provide generally spin-free perspectives, are suffering. The evening newscasts on ABC, CBS and NBC; the entire CNN cable network; magazines such as *Time*, and many general-interest newspapers, are losing out to competitors who specialize in spin.

Today, the hottest blogs, radio shows, and cable-TV channels are those for which fact is merely a four-letter word.

It's worth noting that mainstream news distribution remains huge in the U.S., with as many as 25 million viewers for the three network newscasts, and over 40 million newspapers printed each day, containing opinion pages that continue to provide a healthy range of views.

But the nation's spin cycle is gaining speed.

Spinning too fast makes you dizzy, and being dizzy causes you to lose your balance.

MEDIA 2.0

Steal This Video

Back in 1971 when the hippie revolution's Pied Piper, Abbie Hoffman, authored "Steal This Book" he got the very outrage he sought. Thirty publishing houses rejected it and, when the book finally came out, more than a dozen newspapers refused to print ads to promote it.

According to Hoffman's inverted reasoning, it was immoral "to not steal from the institutions that are the pillars of the Pig Empire." His manual included advice on stealing many things—including movies.

Ah, the times and the media are a changin'. But what about the morals?

The title of a column in *The New York Times* Sunday business section (April 7, 2013) read: "No TV? No Subscription? No Problem." It wasn't merely a summary of widespread theft that plagues the entertainment industry in the digital age—a topic covered in many places, including in *The Times*—it was a pro-stealing treatise by a *Times* staffer, Jenna Wortham, that Abbie Hoffman probably couldn't have articulated better himself.

Wortham began by recounting how she and her friends planned to watch HBO's hit drama "Game of Thrones." Only one member of the group would use a valid subscription; the others would each rely on what Wortham described as "a crafty workaround." In her case, that meant stealing the program by using the password of "a guy in New Jersey that I had once met in a Mexican restaurant."

Reporter Wortham even wrote that she "hesitated" before seeking a comment from HBO, fearing that it might prompt "a crackdown" and "I'd become the most-hated person on the Internet."

With 30 million paying subscribers, HBO isn't exactly hurting. In fact, Wortham's "research" led her to conclude that HBO and other video providers "seemed to have little to no interest in curbing our sharing behavior—in part because they can't."

That last bit of phrasing packs quite a wallop. It's beyond Hoffmanesque to describe the theft of proprietary material as "sharing." It's also conveniently misleading to conclude that the entertainment industry is indifferent to being robbed simply because, for the time being at least, there isn't a practical way to stop it.

Content owners in all media, from music to newspapers, have struggled to overcome the perception that the Internet, and everything that flows through it, is inherently "free." Of course it's not, and the media cited have paid dearly for allowing such a faulty premise to take hold for more than a decade, before finally taking steps to correct it.

At least Abbie Hoffman focused on a political objective. He wasn't concerned with getting something for free as much as he was with changing the balance of power in society. And Hoffman's title was ironic since over a quarter of a million people willingly paid for his book, making it a best seller.

HBO, in particular, has frustrated some consumers by declining to offer its mobile app, known as HBO Go, as a standalone product. The only way to get the app is to be a paying subscriber to the regular cable or satellite service. That business decision angers some viewers who feel it is not in the spirit of the digital age.

Wortham believes many media companies fail "to grasp the future of television as a shared social experience online." The buzzwords "shared" and "social experience" seem to overlook the needs of businesses to function as profit-making enterprises, protected from those who would steal their products.

And finally, Wortham had the juice to complain that when she tried to log on illegally to HBO Go, "the site was buckling under the load of many others who, just like me, were tuning in at 10 p.m."

Modern media, especially those with shallower pockets than HBO, have the unenviable task of marketing their material while also convincing potential customers that stealing it is uncool.

"We all mellow with age," Abbie Hoffman told me, 13 years after writing his unlikely best seller. For him, thievery was a means to an end, and not part of a shared social experience.

◆◆◆

The Joke's on Whom?

I've pranked several thousand people, although I never favored that term. Much of my career has been spent doing hidden-camera stunts on "Candid Camera," following a path charted for decades by my father. We always worried about what might go wrong, particularly involving the physical and emotional health of unsuspecting subjects. Our gags were relatively tame, and we sought to find greater social meaning in each sequence. Our track record was pretty good. Still, we had our share of critics.

Tens of millions heard, or heard about, the telephone gag conducted in late 2012 by two Australian radio hosts, who called a hospital in London pretending to be Queen Elizabeth II and Prince Charles. Despite their admittedly awful attempts at British accents, they were transferred to a nurse caring for Kate Middleton, the Duchess of Cambridge, who was hospitalized with severe morning sickness.

The joke seemed harmless, until a few days later when news came that the nurse who answered the call, Jacintha Saldanha, had committed suicide.

This tragic turn quickly triggered debate about practical joking in the digital age, when everything is magnified by the potential for viral distribution.

The practical joking itself—usually on video—has intensified in both volume and crudeness. This is in part a result of desensitizing among viewers, for whom the barrage of clips becomes so overwhelming that it's easy to lose track of the inherent risks involved. People in flash videos are sometimes thought of almost as avatars or digital creations, rather than actual human beings, whose feelings and health are always potentially in jeopardy.

In the case of the nurse's death, it seemed that once again the medium is more to blame than the message. A phone prank confined to those directly involved in the call is not likely to cause much stress. Even a radio broadcast heard only in Australia would not seem too damaging for a "victim" in Britain. But a viral prank that flashes around the globe on radio, TV, the Internet and newspapers can make even a silly joke seem to carry the weight of the world.

The very morning that the news came from London, NBC's "Today" show was replaying for the umpteenth time a clip from Brazil in which people in an elevator were frightened by the unexpected appearance of a ghostly figure—actually a prankster who entered through a secret door. The video, which established a record for views worldwide, had no shred of comedic content beyond the screams, tears and shocked expressions of those caught unawares. If ever a prank posed health risks for its victims, this would seem to be it. But the NBC hosts hooted with laughter.

In my view, the Australian DJs did nothing wrong other than attempt a sophomoric gag that had an awful, but unpredictable, consequence. Yet everything is magnified and made permanent in the digital environment.

Pranksters must always be accountable for their actions, but in the digital age the burden of responsibility also lies with those who use the echo chamber to amplify things to the point of distortion and stress. Unless we're careful, the joke is on us.

◆◆◆

April What?

I'm often asked if folks are more difficult to trick today. After all, we're all so dialed in and media savvy, you'd think we would be less susceptible to jokes—practical or otherwise.

Fact is, people are more easily tricked than ever.

Multi-tasking has a lot to do with it; hardly any moments remain when we focus our complete attention on just one thing. We're easily distracted, and any magician will tell you that distraction is the key to fooling people. Also, technology has made such incredible leaps that almost anything seems possible, and thus believable.

But the perfect storm for chicanery is in media. Ease of access via the Internet, coupled with speedy distribution that leaves fact-checkers in the dust, is creating a robust market for fake news—if you like that sort of thing. How difficult can it be to fool Americans at a time when an alarming percentage of them tell pollsters they use Jon Stewart's "Daily Show" as a primary source for news?

Among the gems: a report that Paul Krugman, the *New York Times* columnist and Nobel winner in economics, had filed for bankruptcy. The item was written by a satirical website called The Daily Currant and then transmitted as real news by the financial blog Prudent Investor via Boston.com (owned by *The Times*) and picked up by the conservative site Breitbart.com.

The Currant struck a few weeks earlier with a bogus story that Sarah Palin was joining the Middle Eastern news service Al Jazeera. *The Washington Post's* Suzi Parker reported it as fact, prompting Palin to tweet, "Hey @washingtonpost, I'm having coffee with Elvis this week."

This might be fun, except for what it says about our politics and our news. We increasingly rely on the Internet to reinforce our beliefs, so we naturally grab at things that appear to do that. We're so enamored of click-and-share gossip that we pass things along without much question. Even the largest media outlets seem eager to link to the juiciest items that are "trending."

Media were so hungry for tidbits about Pope Francis that not one but several phony Twitter accounts were cited at various times as being the new pope's true messages, until the Vatican cleared things up.

The public may be as gullible as ever, but it's also media professionals who are falling for the phony news stories. That's nothing new—it's just that hoaxsters now have better tools.

Back in the early 80s I wrote an annual April Fools column in which I sought to fool media with fake news about media. One year, shortly after singer Michael Jackson accidentally burned some of his hair during a pyrotechnic stunt, I wrote that Paramount was making a movie about it called "Tingle," and that MTV had paid millions for the video, while USA Network was preparing a "Tingle" workout show and Parker Bros. was selling a "Tingle" board game. I even said Allstate was handling fire insurance for the entire "Tingle" enterprise.

Richard Hack, a writer for the trade publication *Hollywood Reporter*, went on national TV to break the "news." To his discredit, he didn't even name his source for the story, claiming the reporting to be his own.

I finally gave up writing April Fools columns after concluding that media types were so easily gulled it just wasn't fun to mess with them.

Now websites like The Daily Currant and The Onion do this sort of thing as a business. The public is occasionally tricked, but it's media that increasingly play the fools.

◆ ◆ ◆

Viewing or Gorging?

I spent part of my vacation overdosing on the TV series "Homeland." This meant viewing all 24 episodes in a three-day period, watching several a second time, digging up print reviews and features I had ignored over the previous two years—plus a few more obsessive gambits, such as searching for the Israeli series on which the Showtime hit is based.

This type of famine or feast approach to media is not new for me, but it's probably not what the producers have in mind. I do find that more and more people are either fully into things these days, or completely out of them. We have so many entertainment options, yet few of us enjoy sampling; we latch on to something we like at the media buffet and then gorge.

At least "Homeland" references now make sense, most notably the "Saturday Night Live" sketch I went back and watched online. Turns out Bill Hader's "Saul" and Anne Hathaway's "Carrie" were among the funniest send-ups SNL has ever done.

What's that? You've never watched "Homeland"? The way I figure it, that places you among roughly 300 million Americans.

"Homeland" is a thriller about the CIA's post-9/11 efforts to wipe out Al Qaeda, featuring almost as many plot twists as, well, the real CIA. It's one of television's biggest hits, but unlike, say, "American Idol," which has been sampled at one time or another by virtually everyone who owns a TV, "Homeland" has been seen by a tiny fraction of the U.S. audience.

Roughly 2 million people watched the second season's finale. By comparison, over 30 million tuned in the Cowboys-Redskins game on NBC two weeks later. Still, when it comes to the zeitgeist, "Homeland" is right up there with the NFL.

President Obama told *People Magazine* that "Homeland" is one of his favorite shows, and the Clintons are also said to be big fans. In 2012, the program's male lead, Damian Lewis, was invited to the White House for a chat with Mr. Obama about where the plot might lead.

I missed the "Homeland" debut in 2011, and found myself trapped. I was afraid to join the series in mid-story, so I managed to avoid it altogether. But for Christmas I received the first season on

DVD, and my son Danny and I—who together once watched all 154 episodes of NBC's "The West Wing," three times from start to finish, after the series was no longer on the air—polished off the first 12 "Homeland" shows in less than 48 hours.

Locating the second season was tougher. I pre-ordered the DVDs on Amazon.com and then realized I had no idea when they'd be released. I signed up for a one-month trial of Netflix, only to find out it doesn't offer "Homeland." Fortunately, there's an app called Showtime Anytime, which I downloaded to my iPad, and then rushed to the Apple store for a cable that would let me watch iPad video on a full-size TV.

However, it seems Showtime won't allow that. While the show played perfectly on the iPad, a printed notice on the TV screen said I was not allowed to watch on a separate TV monitor. Still, we watched episodes 13 through 24 on the small device in a day-and-a-half.

That done, I began Googling the Israeli series, "Hatufim," (Abductees) and learned that it exists on DVD with English subtitles—but to watch it I'd have to buy a machine that accommodates the TV format called PAL, used widely outside the U.S. Instead, I spent $24.99 on Amazon, plus rush shipping, for a movie called "Homeland," which I discovered has absolutely nothing to do with the TV series. It's about an Israeli soldier named Kobi who comes to New York, where he meets Leila, and...oh, who cares. I guess I was thrown by reading that the film had won an award, which I later discovered was bestowed by the Delray Beach Film Festival.

Anyway, I raced into the New Year fully prepped to discuss "Homeland," only to find that those who have seen it are already talked-out, and the other 300 million couldn't care less. It seems the buzz has shifted. I hear that two seasons of "Downton Abbey" are available on DVD.

Meanwhile, Netflix took gorging to a whole new level by releasing 13 episodes of its drama "House of Cards" all at once. The company was pretty much daring viewers like me to pull an all-nighter and consume the series in one sitting. I'm afraid that's the same as someone giving me a year's subscription to the Candy of the Month Club—then announcing that all 12 boxes will be delivered on the same day.

♦ ♦ ♦

Chatter Box

Talk is cheap, and that's one explanation for why a new type of innocuous, chatty, talk programming is spreading quickly on mainstream television.

The more significant reason, however, is that the format is an extension of what is happening in new digital media—a process that could be called *chatter box syndrome*.

The model for this type of program is "The View," ABC's coffee klatch gathering of celebrity women, led by Barbara Walters, which has been around since 1997. Although successful, and replicated in other countries, "The View" did not spawn many U.S. imitators until recently. Then, with almost the viral speed known to the Internet, the format popped up on dozens of broadcast and cable outlets.

CBS has an almost identical program called "The Talk." Fox News Channel offers "The Five" and "Red Eye." MSNBC came up with "The Cycle," and CNN briefly tried in its prime-time schedule a gab fest called "(Get to) The Point," which was only distinguishable from the raft of similar programs by its title—and, then, barely so. Just about every network, from ESPN to Bravo, has introduced shows devoted to lowbrow chitchat.

Existing programs have also implemented the format, including Sean Hannity's "The Great American Panel" on Fox News, and "The Professionals" on NBC's "Today" show.

Talk programming is nothing new on TV—in fact, it's been a staple since the earliest days. What's different is that the newer chat shows don't often bother with guests or "experts"; rather, they rely on a permanent roster of B-list panelists, whom viewers get to know much as they do the cast of the "Real Housewives."

It wasn't long ago that most "talking heads" were anathema to television programmers, except in the wee hours and on Sunday mornings. So what changed?

For one thing, there's the Fluff Factor. During stressful economic and social times, many viewers are worn out by serious problems for which there seem to be no solutions. They use social media to dwell on smaller issues—and they enjoy watching groups of their TV "friends" chatting about the same innocuous things.

Julie Chen, host of "The Talk," calls her program "a support group for women out there"—what one critic quickly termed, "virtual girlfriends for people who don't have real ones." Or, perhaps, folks whose friends are only on Facebook.

The tabloid topics that provide fodder for chat TV are the ones showcased minute-to-minute on the home pages of Yahoo and AOL as well as on TMZ, Twitter and Google. It's the "hot topic" of the moment—be it Kate Middleton's outfits or the latest winner on "The Voice."

Even when the chatterazzi turn to meaningful areas like politics, they tend to overdose on the more sensational issues. And like the Internet, TV kibitzing rarely shapes opinions; it only tends to reinforce views through verbal mastication.

That such slender formats can gain popularity on TV underscores the basic loneliness in the digital age, along with the growing preference for softer, less threatening themes.

The trend in talk TV, where harshness is yielding to sappiness—as with Fox's replacement of the bombastic Glenn Beck with "The Five"—is mirrored by "reality" programming, where innocuous song and dance competitions now attract more viewers than insect-eating contests once did.

The sad thing about chat TV, with its virtual friends from Hollywood's and Washington's B lists, is that it's no more "real" than reality TV. As entertainment, it's harmless. But CNN, which viewers still consider a serious news alternative, wisely declared it's new show DOA, leaving the channel's core audience to wonder, what exactly was the point?

◆◆◆

Lipstick Commentary

This may not be politically correct, but it's politically intriguing: Increasingly on television, the more conservative women are in their views, the more liberal they are in flaunting their sexuality.

Television favors attractive people, both women and men, regardless of their politics—that's a given. But when it comes to female hosts and commentators, there is an unmistakable difference between the way conservatives dress and are shown on camera as compared to their liberal counterparts.

The numerous examples include Kimberly Guilfoyle, the severely made-up, short-skirted analyst on Fox News Channel, and Andrea Tantaros, her equally provocative co-host on the political talk show "The Five." When MSNBC launched a competing program called "The Cycle," it hired as its lone conservative S. E. Cupp, the articulate Cornell graduate who, in her previous role at Fox, was known for delivering commentaries with her legs propped salaciously on the anchor desk.

The issue isn't brains or beauty. Most of cable-TV's women, across the political spectrum, have plenty of both. It's about style, image and, make no mistake about it, deliberate packaging decisions by TV producers.

Sarah Palin helped create the model, and Fox News has been largely responsible for advancing it. To some viewers it creates an apparent contradiction between on-screen imagery and basic conservative social standards.

Cupp blames the media establishment for making females' appearance an issue. "The liberal media always has a difficult time dealing with pretty, conservative women," she said, prior to joining MSNBC. "They just don't know what to make of it."

But what is it about the conservative audience that seems to prefer its female commentators dressed like they're headed to a cocktail party, while progressive viewers favor more subdued business attire? What are producers really aiming for when they calculatingly place Guilfoyle and Cupp in what studio crews call the "leg chair," insuring that viewers can ogle them from head to toe?

In the prescient political drama "The West Wing" Emily Proctor played an overtly sexy Republican lawyer, working among generally plain-Jane Democrats in Jed Bartlet's White House. "I don't think whatever sexuality I have diminishes my power," Ainsley Hayes tells female colleagues. "I think it enhances it." The phenomenon is known as "lipstick feminism" and "stiletto feminism."

Whatever you call it, it's on display across the dial. There's Elizabeth Hasselbeck, the conservative with cover-girl looks on "The View," and Ann Coulter, the commentator who isn't particularly modest in promoting her opinion or appearance.

The flashy style preference among conservative women is a recurrent topic on Internet blogs. Lori Ziganto, once named one of the "20 Hottest Conservative Women in New Media," writes: "We embrace all aspects of our gender. As such, we have no problem looking pretty whilst vivisecting you verbally in an argument." She adds, "we know that if one appreciates how you look, it doesn't preclude them from also appreciating your mind and your political discourse."

The televangelist Rev. Jim Osborne blogs: "I have noticed that Conservative/Republican women all seem to be very attractive while the Liberal/Democrat types are just God-awful ugly. Why is that?" Osborne's theory: "Ugly women are angry at God for creating them that way, so they choose to rebel against God and embrace atheism and liberalism. The converse is true for attractive women."

Apparently the issue of style and appearance has become as contentious in social media—including cable—as politics itself. Osborne's ridiculous invective aside, women on TV seem divided on the very definition of feminism. Conservatives almost dare viewers to take them any less seriously because of their flashy appearance, while progressives see the superficial matter of style as a distraction.

Producers tend to favor whatever attracts viewers, and sexy commentators do attract a fringe audience, largely male, that tunes in for the visual stimulation. Conservatives are able to take advantage of this bonus because their core audience doesn't find it objectionable; liberals would appreciate the bonus but correctly assume that a majority of viewers would reject it.

Conservative women on TV—at least those willing to play along—are able to have their cheesecake without eating their words too.

◆◆◆

LOW TECH

App Seeks Your Vote

Eyeing the billion-dollar political market, I am today unveiling a Campaign Speech app for iPhones. I've invited reporters to watch and listen as the app is programmed with the following menu options. Candidate: middle-aged, male, Republican. Office sought: U.S. Congress. Venue: Ohio. Veracity Level: low.

Here is a transcript of the app's remarks:

Hello, Toledo! Thank you! It's...it's great to be back in the state that my mom's uncle once proudly called home!

I share your concerns, and that's why I have a 12-point plan.

We need good, decent jobs for good, decent Americans—the hard-working good, decent folks who seek their small slice of the American Dream. It's the dream my grandfather had when he arrived at Ellis Island, with only the clothes on his back and the passion in his heart.

My grandpa had big hands. He was a produce unpacker: a guy who opened heavy boxes of produce at the grocery store, tossed the rotten pieces on the damp, sticky floor, and carried the boxes to aisles where skilled union workers arranged the fruit and vegetables in tall, artful displays. Grandpa hated unions. He also hated produce and developed rashes on both hands, but you know what? He never once whined about not having health insurance.

He didn't give up. He didn't give up because he had a dream that someday his grandson would stand before you with a dream for a brighter America.

My dad ran off when I was just 3. I won't apologize for him, and I won't ever apologize for the United States of America!

Mom and I lived with a small troupe of circus performers in a musty trailer. I did my schoolwork at a table fashioned from an old wagon wheel. You could see right through the spokes to the floor of the trailer. And you could see right through holes in the floor to the muddy ground below...and right through a hole in the ground to an area where elephant droppings collected.

Friends, my story is part of the rich history we all share as Americans. It's what makes us exceptional.

God gave us our exceptionalism, and politicians can't take it away. But the mainstream media...those who'd like to do your thinking for you...they'll never tell you that.

When I was 24, mom won $3.6 million in the lottery. She was a winner! And America doesn't need a government that picks winners and losers.

We gave mom's money to a firm that manages investments for circus employees, and a few weeks later they made me an executive vice president. I learned about business in the real world.

As mom always said, "If you have no particular skill or education, you can still live lavishly in America by controlling other people's money."

My fellow Americans, mom never had a safety net. Others, like those who performed on the high wire did, of course, but my mom...toiling in the circus costume shop, where she made bootstraps for the performers who wore boots...she never had a net.

Has America lost her way? Manufacturing jobs are going to China, and good, decent circus positions are being grabbed by immigrants, who may very well be here illegally. I have a plan to change that.

My opponent believes we can tax our way to a better tomorrow...and spend our way to a better day-after tomorrow...and then, the next day, raise taxes and, two days later, spend even more. My plan will put us back on track!

In the words of Ronald Reagan as he quoted Abraham Lincoln many years ago, "The shining light of America's great promise burns brightest for those who shine brightly from within."

The time is now! This is our moment! Dare to dream, and never fail to dream a dare!

God bless you! God bless the United States of America! God bless you all! And God bless my lovely wife, Siri.

◆◆◆

Voice Lessons

Back in the '80s our family had a Chrysler station wagon with limited vocabulary and laughably stilted pronunciation. We'd jump in and the car would declare in a halting voice, "A...door...is...a... jar." That made us laugh, and it prompted my sister to quip, "I always thought a door was a toaster."

Dad's car was easy to live with because it didn't have a human name, and it never talked back.

Now, many of my friends can't go more than a few miles without checking with Siri, the fawning female who resides in iPhones and iPads. Even if you don't own the devices you've undoubtedly seen TV commercials in which Siri flirts with a young musician and coos, "I will call you Rock Star."

These voices have been creeping up on us for some time. I used to look forward to hearing the "You've got mail" guy at AOL—who peaked around the time he starred in a movie with Meg Ryan and Tom Hanks—but lately he seems out of touch.

Several companies now use the phone voice I first heard at United Airlines: the guy who cheerfully repeats the same questions over and over, apparently hoping you'll hang up in frustration before reaching an actual person, probably in the Philippines. You feel like you've won some sort of contest when he finally says, "OK. I'll get an agent for ya!"

What strikes me as a cruel twist is that the presumably live offshore operators seem to be trained to speak English just like robots.

I'm fascinated by the sheer endurance of the airport woman who spends the day repeating eight gloomy words: "The moving sidewalk is coming to an end."

I feel kind of sorry for my old answering machine who's so senile it takes her forever just to spit out, "End...of...messages."

I was surprised to discover that my Mac computer can read whatever is on my screen in 100 different voices, each of which Apple has thoughtfully given a human name. The default guy is Alex, but right now I'm listening to Serena—who I imagine is 5-foot-10 with long dark hair—reading this piece with her sultry British accent.

The first machine to really give me the heebie-jeebies was Watson, the I.B.M. smarty-pants who beat people named Brad and Ken on

"Jeopardy." Watson sat there smugly, using his ultra-speedy buzzer capability and lightening recall to win more than three times his nearest human competitor.

What's next? Melvin, the talking toothbrush ("Don't forget to scrub your tongue"). Hank, the grouchy lawnmower ("Gotta do something about those gophers"). Sally, the nagging refrigerator ("Save some of that blueberry pie for tomorrow, Tubby").

A company called Zazu is marketing a mobile alarm clock that wakes you with a female voice delivering not only the time but also news and weather—even details of what your friends are saying on social networks. The Zazu lady also reads a commercial, something I suspect was a human's bright idea.

The football star Payton Manning is seen in a commercial talking to his Buick as he drives. And Audi vehicles come with a "multimedia interface" on the dashboard that fields spoken questions from drivers. Audi says it is working on a system that recognizes and adapts to the motorist's state of mind to determine if the driver is stressed by a traffic situation.

Personally, I'm stressed when a gadget talks to me, no matter how bad the traffic happens to be. I continue to believe that machines should be seen but not heard.

◆◆◆

BRUSHES WITH NATURE

Porcini Parade

PEBBLE BEACH, Calif.—Across the street are three young men carrying cloth sacks, walking slowly through the woods in hunched-over style—a posture known in south Florida as the Sanibel Stoop, because Sanibel Island's gorgeous shells lure many beachcombers. But here in Central California the bounty is a tasty brown mushroom, so you might say this is the Porcini Parade.

A dozen or more foragers trekked by this morning, remarkable when you consider that here in the Del Monte Forest I wouldn't expect to see that many passersby in a month. Usually, cars are only parked on the sides of these roads during major golf tournaments, but since mushroom fever struck in November they're wedged under trees and leaning into ditches, as their owners poke for porcinis.

Perhaps it was the early fall rain and favorable temperatures that moved Mother Nature to make this the best porcini season in anyone's memory. Maybe it was the sour economy that inspired so many folks to pay the fee to enter this renowned tourist venue, and then skip the scenic drive in favor of searching for pudgy mushrooms that retail for as much as $10 apiece.

An acquaintance for whom an hour of searching in past years sometimes led to a phone call with the news, "I found one!" reports this season she has 186 porcinis in her freezer.

Two young men parked near my house last week and boasted they had a thousand dollars worth of orders from restaurants in San Francisco. Indeed, the back of their car was crammed with perfect Boletus edulis specimens, some with caps as wide as Frisbees.

Encouraged by my wife Amy, who is a great cook but not a nature-lover, I took up the hunt. I managed to make every possible mistake—from using a plastic bag (it makes the porcinis "sweat"), to washing off the dirt rather than using a dry brush (they suck up the water and rot).

I got poison oak on my face, cut my left hand in two places, and twisted an ankle tripping over a downed tree. Yet, it was exhilarating.

After a few weeks in the forest our dinner conversation began to sound like the scene from "Forrest Gump" in which Bubba obsesses about uses for shrimp. "You can barbecue it, boil it, broil it, bake it, sauté it..." But regardless of your culinary creativity, there are only so many ways to cook porcinis.

So I placed an ad on Craig's List offering "Grade AA" porcinis for $12 a pound. Soon I got a call from a woman who fit the necessary profile: she loves mushrooms but had been out of town since the harvest began, and wasn't aware that this year porcinis are so plentiful they're probably growing in her driveway. She paid me $20 for six smallish specimens.

Next I went to the fanciest restaurant in town, where the chef estimated I was the 25th porcini seller to come by. Nevertheless, he paid me $50 for a seven-pound bag.

The moral of this story—not the morel, because that's an entirely different type of mushroom—probably has something to do with weather, economy, nature, human nature and capitalism. However, I can't quite figure out which.

I recall my mother reminding me on dozens of occasions that "money doesn't grow on trees." She never talked about the times when it pokes out from under pine needles.

Anyway, mushroom season is ending. The woods look like a battlefield, with rutted earth and scattered carcasses of mushrooms that were ripped from the ground and then found to be either spoiled or the wrong variety. Foragers are hanging up their Boletus brushes, wondering if this bounty will occur again next fall.

Diehard scavengers will now turn from nature's exquisite plan to duffers' errant shots. The woods here provide hiding places for thousands of misplaced golf balls, some worth a buck or two at local golf shops. They can be found by anyone caring to do the Titleist Trot.

◆ ◆ ◆

Rambunctious Raccoons

Our backyard is filled with the pleasing sounds of spring created by birds, frogs, crickets—and teens down the street testing their new cars. But lately there are also the haunting sounds of raccoons laughing at me.

When we moved in 18 years ago, I wondered why neighbors were so protective of their trash that they secured garbage cans with fancy bungee cords and even padlocks.

Word apparently spread through the raccoon community that my trashcans were left unlocked at the curb. After dark the biggest raccoons would push the cans over, the juniors would pull off the lids, and the little ones would gobble my wife's leftovers, while resolutely scattering everything else across the road.

Eventually, I drilled holes in the cans and installed industrial strength locks. It's quite a sight on collection days, watching the garbage men struggling to open so many protective devices just to dump the trash.

We'd been mercifully raccoon-free until a few months ago when I walked out one morning and discovered that our lawn was pretty much dismantled. If you haven't seen what a team of raccoons can do to a lawn, imagine a bunch of huge sardine cans, each about three feet long, with the lids peeled back. Or, imagine a dozen bald heads, each about three feet wide, with toupees pulled off and tossed to the side. Or, imagine some gigantic prehistoric golfer making three-foot long divots.

These are the images that haunted me every night. In the morning I'd go out and close the huge flaps of grass and stomp them down, seeking to avoid permanent damage.

Eventually I had to hire a lawn guy. "You've got raccoons," he announced, with the same smugness I recall my dentist using when he told me I had impacted wisdom teeth. What he failed to mention before selling me high-priced replacement sod is that new turf doesn't discourage raccoons, it actually attracts them. My raccoons apparently prefer it to old, chewed-over grass.

This discovery led me to the hardware store, where Ernie explained my options. You can shoot 'em (out of the question); poison 'em (equally unacceptable), or trap 'em.

The trap I bought is rather plush—in fact I once sat next to a woman on a four-hour plane ride who had her cat in a far less comfortable looking container. The trick, of course, is to persuade a raccoon to go inside. "They'll eat anything," Ernie assured me. Anything, it turns out, except garbage. I baited my trap with the very same type of garbage that raccoons had knocked over trashcans to get, and they wouldn't touch it. So I began experimenting with raccoon cuisine, resulting in a tempting assortment of peanut butter sandwiches, honey-covered apples and chocolate cookies. A nightly refrain in our kitchen was, "Don't touch that! It's for the raccoons."

One morning I discovered we had a rather fat but otherwise clean raccoon in our trap. Impulsively, I grabbed my camera and photographed him, although I have no idea why.

Seems that once the sun comes up, and after digesting several peanut butter sandwiches, raccoons are fairly subdued. I drove the raccoon, in his comfy airline-quality carrier, to a wooded area about three miles away.

The next night I caught his friend. Then his friend's friend. And this continued until a total of five raccoons of various sizes, each dutifully photographed, had been relocated to other neighborhoods.

For the next few weeks my lawn flourished, and the humongous divots healed. Then, at about 3 a.m. one morning, our dog Dottie bounded off the bed and began barking furiously. The lights on the deck revealed three raccoons, leaning against a wooden chair, grinning.

Now I'm back to making peanut butter sandwiches and carpooling raccoons across town. I'm sleep-deprived, worrying about craters in the lawn.

Recently, while releasing my catch, a guy drove up and asked what I was doing. I explained that I lived a few miles away and was trying to move this critter to a safe area, far enough away from my house that he wouldn't return.

"We have raccoon problems of our own," he said. "I wish you wouldn't bring yours here." He said he knew of a perfect spot—a place where he's been releasing his raccoons for several months.

As he spoke, it became clear that the area he was describing was about a block-and-a-half from my house.

During all this, the raccoon I had released a few minutes earlier was clinging to the side of a nearby pine tree. I'm absolutely certain he was laughing.

Watch Your Step When Traveling

After spending the night at one of the major hotel chains recently and finding an unwelcome surprise behind a chair in the corner, I realize the true meaning of the term "pet peeve." It means I'm peeved at the way many hotels are loosening their policies about pets.

Now, hold on, animal lovers. I love my dog. I've loved all five cats that I rescued and cared for. And I love that more doors are opening to you and your pet. I just don't want to walk in after you and step in something.

According to a national poll, roughly 10 million Americans travel with pets every year. That figure is likely to have climbed as economic stress made some people vacation closer to home—meaning they would drive rather than fly, and were more likely to bring along a dog or cat.

The "U.S. Pet Ownership & Demographics Sourcebook" (don't ask; I never heard of it either) reports, "more than half of U.S. pet owners say their pets are part of the family." That factoid was picked up and used as the opening sentence of a press release in which Hilton Hotels announced a special pet friendly program, including "pet concierge service."

The Hilton statement gushed about pet-friendly rooms loaded with "upscale amenities sure to please the most pampered dog or cat." The decor is by William Wegman, known for his images of Weimaraners clothed in human garb—although never, to my knowledge, in diapers. Pet services will include "a stain-, water-, and microbial-resistant pet bed, as well as food and water bowls with placemat, and an exclusive pet amenity kit."

My dog Dottie long ago traded her bed for the one my wife and I share. So, with due respect to Wegman, I believe Hilton's pet beds will not only resist stains, they'll resist pets, too, as long as there's a bed for humans nearby.

At Westin, dogs are now offered "Heavenly Beds," made with Westin's "signature white-on-white stripe pattern fabric," available to take home for only $225. Again, my dog may be in the minority here, but she sees to it that anything white-on-white becomes mud-on-white within minutes.

Many hotels are adding pet food to menus. Loews Hotels now offers "Bow Wow Tenderloin of Beef," made with filet mignon, eggs, brown rice, and bread. I believe my dog would rather stay home and chew on an old slipper.

The increase in the number of people determined to travel with pets has led to the creation of the website Pets-Allowed-Hotels.com. In a review, Jennifer notes that she stayed at a La Quinta Inn with her boxer, and the hotel was very accommodating about the barking. Sandra stayed with her dog at a Residence Inn and was charged a $100 cleaning fee. "Wow," she writes, "that's more than I pay to have my entire house cleaned!"

Maggie Gallant, host of Animal Planet's "Pet Trends," was asked by Via magazine about trends in pet travel. She says that her dachshund, Dixie, now favors "aromatherapy." She adds, "If Dixie gets nervous at security, I give her a spray of lavender, a natural essence that relaxes both people and pets."

Sad to say, if you were to follow my dog into a hotel room, the aroma would never make you think lavender.

What concerns me, now that hotels have determined that catering to pets is the latest marketing battleground, is what seasoned travelers call the "ick factor." There's plenty of it, even at the best hotels: those hairs in the shower, the used tissue in the desk drawer, the sticky stuff on the phone. Add the natural substances that come with pets of all shapes and sizes, and there is reason to fear increased hotel ickiness.

All the major chains have detailed policy statements about how they intend to diligently deal with pet ick to ensure that human guests will not suffer. But frankly, even the clean-shower policy doesn't always find its way to the staff swabbing the bathrooms.

Although she would prefer to come with us, Dottie is staying close to home this summer, at a friendly kennel. They don't have Heavenly Beds or amenity kits. But the policy is clear: No people allowed.

Nothing to Crow About

Two crows were in the road. The older bird was dead; the younger, we'll call him Frankie, was standing guard and wouldn't budge.

I moved the dead bird off the pavement hoping the little guy would follow. But Frankie, about three or four weeks old and unable to fly, held his ground. So I took him home, and soon found myself rethinking my view about charities—specifically those dedicated to helping animals rather than humans.

Here's the backstory: I once wrote a column in *USA Today* about people who donate to good causes—the school volleyball team, the animal shelter, etc.—while so many Americans are hungry. We give roughly $300 billion to charities each year, but only 10 percent goes directly to social and human services.

I wasn't criticizing the well-intentioned efforts of any particular charity, but suggested that donors should apply a triage system at this time of profound human need.

I put Frankie in a large box, and Googled "caring for young crows and ravens."

Seems these birds make good pets, provided they are introduced to people before being "imprinted" in the wild. I also learned that they're quite messy, often moody, and will eat just about anything. One site said for youngsters you must "place a glob of food on your finger and push it down the crow's throat." I wish I had video of my failed attempts at doing this for Frankie.

My wife Amy suggested I phone the ASPCA, sending me into immediate panic. What if someone there had read my column and labeled me a non-believer? What if Frankie wound up being euthanized in a dingy back room, where I envisioned all the "lesser" critters went eventually?

Kate, in the Wildlife Department, was surprisingly sympathetic. She said one of her colleagues was only a few miles from my house and could be over in a few minutes. She'd come to me? In a few minutes? Good luck getting such service from a plumber.

Jen arrived in a very official-looking truck and put on surgical gloves. She gave Frankie a thorough exam and pronounced him fit, but too underfed to be returned to the wild.

So Jen took Frankie to the ASPCA, where he'll be eating a mixture of cat food and raw vegetables. When stronger, he'll be brought back to the woods near my house.

I was feeling embarrassed about my earlier column, and mumbled something to Jen about sending a donation, which she politely said wasn't necessary.

In the column I asked, "If you encountered a starving child holding a starving puppy, would your first step be to offer food to the dog? Obviously not." I still agree with that—as would Kate and Jen, I imagine.

But maybe it's not so simple. All living things deserve our sympathetic attention, especially those who, by chance, are placed in our paths.

Years ago I was driving up Madison Avenue in New York when a scrawny kitten ran under my car. I stopped and got out, blocking the busy intersection at rush hour. The crowd quickly divided into two camps: those who yelled, "Get moving!" and those who screamed, "It's right under your car!"

That cat—later named Dasher because during the hourlong drive that followed he managed to crawl behind the dashboard, requiring the services of an auto mechanic to free him—racked up $1,300 in vet bills. A ridiculous expenditure, I suppose. But that's something else about "lesser" creatures in our lives: once you reach out to them, their problems become yours.

The ASPCA, founded in 1866, operates under the belief that "animals are entitled to kind and respectful treatment at the hands of humans." While I waited for Jen and Frankie to return, I sent a modest donation.

The wordsmith in me wants to say I was forced to eat crow, but the creature-lover in me would rather not.

Humans Should LOL

I don't recall ever writing LOL in an email or text—although I will occasionally place the symbols ":)" in a message to make clear I'm just joshing.

Fact is, laughing out loud is one of the healthiest things we can do. A hearty laugh exercises the lungs and releases beneficial endorphins. Besides, it feels good.

I worry, though, that many who type LOL on the computer or mobile device aren't really laughing much at all. I picture them alone in their rooms or a coffee shop, sending the message without ever cracking a smile. I used to get that same reaction from certain network executives after I proudly showed them my best TV footage. "That's funny," they'd say absolutely straight-faced, "really funny."

The point is, you've got to train yourself to laugh freely, to really let loose.

Let me tell you about the best laugh I ever had. I was working a 4 a.m. shift in a newsroom in Peekskill, N.Y., and as the first one in it was my job to unlock the place and get things going.

One morning, in my bleary state, I noticed a folded sheet of paper on the boss's desk, and on it was written: "Confidential."

I tried to keep walking, I really did, but finally I was compelled to take a peek. I gently lifted the paper and saw a message that read: "Good morning, Peter!"

All alone in that cavernous room I laughed—no, I roared—aloud for several minutes. It was the funniest thing that ever happened to me, and yet there wasn't a soul around to see or hear it.

Actually, that's one of the marks of a great practical joke: the perpetrator sets the trap with such cunning that he doesn't even have to witness the results. It just works.

So for those of us who wish to retain our cautious optimism, my advice is to LOL whenever possible. But don't just type it, do it!

ACKNOWLEDGEMENTS

Much of the research and fact-checking for this project was done by my colleague Brian Courrejou, to whom I am grateful. At the Candid Camera office, Lesley Konya is a key asset on any project.

Along with my wife Amy, editing help was supplied by my friend Clarence Fanto, a columnist and reporter with the *Berkshire Eagle* in Massachusetts. In the field of book publishing, few people know more than my friend since grade school, Mike Shatzkin. My mother, Evelyn Funt, always supplies the inspiration.

When first presented as op-ed columns, these pieces passed through the hands of many skilled and supportive editors—among them, George Kalogerakis at *The New York Times*, Mark Lasswell and Howard Dickman at *The Wall Street Journal*, and Marjorie Pritchard at *The Boston Globe*.

At my local daily, *The Monterey County Herald*, editor Royal Calkins has provided valuable guidance and encouragement.

The cartoons in this book were supplied by the Cagle Cartoon Syndicate, where Daryl Cagle and the executive editor, Cari Dawson Bartley, aided my shift from hard news to opinion writing.

Speaking of transitions, it's a lucky parent whose kids are able to move from taking advice to providing it—with grace and insight. So I'm fortunate to have Stephanie and Danny on my team. —*P.F.*

PETER FUNT

In one way or another throughout his career, Peter Funt has sought to carry on the Funt Family tradition of making people smile, while examining the human condition.

After 20 years hosting the landmark TV series "Candid Camera," Peter turned to writing op-eds for publications such as *The Wall Street Journal* and *New York Times* as well as his weekly column, distributed by the Cagle Syndicate.

His writing and public appearances contain the same pointed social observations that have made "Candid Camera" so popular since its creation by Peter's dad, Allen, back in 1947.

Peter is a frequent speaker before business and civic groups, using the vast "Candid Camera" library to bring his points to life. His newest presentation, "Six Decades of Smiles," draws upon many years of people-watching, to make audiences think and smile.

Peter and Dorothy beginning their day at 5:45 a.m.

Peter Funt made his first appearance on "Candid Camera" when he and the legendary series were each just three years old. Peter posed as a shoeshine boy who charged $10 per shoe! Over the years he has appeared in hundreds of "Candid Camera" sequences and hosted over 200 network episodes.

In addition to his hidden-camera work, Peter Funt has produced and hosted TV specials on the Arts & Entertainment and Lifetime cable networks. He also spent five years as an editor and reporter with the ABC Radio Network in New York.

Peter was editor and publisher of the national television magazine *On Cable*. He authored the book "Gotcha!" for Grosset & Dunlap on the lost art of practical joking. Peter's essay on the evolution of television is included in "The Story of American Business," published in 2009 by Harvard Business Press.

Peter follows in his father's footsteps as President of Laughter Therapy Foundation, a non-profit organization started by Allen Funt in 1982. Drawing from the "Candid Camera" library, Laughter Therapy sends special videos, at no charge, to critically ill people throughout the United States.

Peter received his degree in journalism from the University of Denver. In 2010 he returned to the Denver campus to be honored as a Master Scholar in Arts and Humanities, and in 2011 was the keynote speaker at the annual Alumni Symposium.

He is a past winner of the Silurian's Award for radio news reporting, for his ABC News coverage of racial disturbances in Asbury Park, N.J., and a recipient of the 2001 Angel Award for television.

Peter is founder of the Monterey County Young Journalists program in California, which provides hands-on training for high school students pursuing careers in news. He also inaugurated the Courtroom Journalism competition in Monterey County in conjunction with the Lyceum Organization, and conducts a similar statewide event for the Constitutional Rights Foundation in Los Angeles.

Peter resides in Central California. He and his wife, Amy, have two children, Stephanie and Danny. His favorite pastimes are golf, baseball, tennis and people watching.

COMING SOON . . .

Peter Funt's candid look behind the camera as he and his dad produced six decades of TV's original "reality" program. From the book's cover story in which Allen hangs his teenage son from the ceiling, to Peter's encounters with celebrities as well as the folks next door, there's no hiding the fun.